The Ultimate

Breville Smart Air Fryer Oven Pro

Cookbook with Pictures

Easy & Tasty Breville Smart Air Fryer Oven Recipes
for Beginners and Advanced Users

Lorraine Braxton

Contents

Introduction 1

FUNDAMENTALS OF BREVILLE SMART AIR FRYER OVEN

What is the Breville Smart Air Fryer Oven? 2

Benefits of Using Breville Smart Air Fryer Oven 2

Main Functions of Breville Smart Air Fryer Oven 2

Components of Breville Air Fryer Oven 4

Before First Using Instructions 4

Care and Cleaning 5

Troubleshooting 5

4-WEEK DIET PLAN

Week 1 7

Week 2 7

Week 3 8

Week 4 8

CHAPTER 1 BREAKFAST RECIPES

Egg Toast Cups 9

Ham Omelet 9

Broiled Corn 9

Oatmeal Porridge with Strawberries 10

Cheese-Bacon Stuffed Bell Peppers 10

Cream Spinach Pie 10

Cheese Sausage Pizza 11

Baked Potatoes & Bell Peppers 11

Egg Rolls 11

Vanilla Cinnamon Granola 12

Baby Spinach Frittata 12

Cheese Sausage Frittata 12

Potato Protein Burrito 13

Baked Rolls 13

Feta Shakshuka 14

Buttermilk Biscuits 14

Saucy Salmon Fillets 14

Simple Banana Bread 15

Banana Bread Pudding 15

Potato Pancakes 15

Zucchini-Apple Bread 16

Homemade Cheese & Sausage Burritos 16

CHAPTER 2 SNACKS AND APPETIZERS RECIPES

Crispy Chickpeas	17	Tasty Cheese Sticks	21
Mini Sausage Pizzas	17	Homemade Potato Chips	21
Stuffed Red Potatoes	18	Ravioli	22
Spinach Rolls	18	Baked Crackers	22
Easy Plantain Pieces	19	Bacon Wrapped Avocado	22
Jicama Strips	19	Breaded Zucchini Sticks	23
Baked Pumpkin Seeds	19	Chicken Tenders	23
Simple French Fries	20	Breaded Avocado Fries	23
Tasty Cauliflower Fritters	20	Roasted Chickpeas	24
Sweet Potato Chips	20	Exotic Chicken Meatballs	24
Air Fried Potato Pieces	21	Mac & Cheese Balls	24

CHAPTER 3 VEGETABLES AND SIDES RECIPES

Cheese Tomato Halves	25	Parmesan Eggplant	29
Carrots & Turnips	25	Fried Tofu Bites	29
Cheese Broccoli Casserole	25	Onion & Sweet Potato Hash	30
Acorn Squash Slices	26	Pumpkin Pieces	30
Brussels Sprouts	26	Delicious Cauliflower in Buffalo Sauce	30
Fried Tofu Cubes	26	Golden Crispy Onion Rings	31
Herbed Head Cauliflower	27	Parmesan Brussels Sprout	31
Green Beans and Mushrooms	27	Stuffed Mushrooms	31
Spicy Okra Fries	27	Broccoli Gratin	32
Tasty Falafels with Tahini Sauce	28	Breaded Cauliflower Fritters	32
Onion Cauliflower Tacos	28	Cheese Balls	32

CHAPTER 4 FISH AND SEAFOOD RECIPES

Vegetable Tilapia Tacos 33

Chili Tilapia 33

Glazed Salmon Fillets 33

Crab Shrimp Roll 34

Rosemary Baked Salmon 34

Breaded Cod Fillets 35

Cajun Salmon Fillet 35

Panko-Crusted Shrimp 35

Pineapple Roasted Fish 36

Shrimp-Rice Stuffed Peppers 36

Flavorful Tilapia Fillets 37

Cheese Fillets 37

Red Snapper with Lemon Slices 37

Cornmeal-Crusted Catfish Fillets 38

Breaded Flounder Fillets 38

Lemon Shrimp 38

Cod Fillets 39

Cornmeal Squid 39

Breaded Fish Fingers 39

Broiled Lobster Tail 40

Garlic Salmon 40

Jumbo Lump Crab Cakes 40

Dijon Tuna Cakes 41

Fried Mackerel Fillets 41

Breadcrumb-Crusted Flounder Fillets 41

CHAPTER 5 CHICKEN AND POULTRY RECIPES

Fried Crusted Chicken 42

Chicken and Veggies Pot Pie 42

Herbed Turkey Roast 43

Herb Chicken Thighs 43

Dijon Turkey Breast 44

Crispy Spiced Chicken 44

Popcorn Chicken 45

Spicy Chicken Wings 45

Delicious Fried Chicken Wings 48

Herbed Turkey Breast 48

Chicken with Pepper Jelly 46

Chicken Pot Pie 46

Herbed Turkey Breast and Bacon 50

Fried Chicken with Peanut Butter 50

Chicken Breasts 50

Roasted Chicken Thighs 47

Teriyaki Chicken Wings 47

Chicken Breasts with Peppers and Onions 47

Crispy Chicken Strips 49

Chicken Parmigiana 49

Turkey Thighs 49

CHAPTER 6 BEEF, PORK, AND LAMB RECIPES

Tasty Spaghetti Squash	51	Sirloin Steaks	56
Pork Tenderloin with Peach Salsa	51	Mini Beef Burger	56
Simple Lamb Roast	52	Cubed Steak	57
Ribeye Steak	52	Delicious Pork Chops	57
Roasted Round Beef	52	Pork Ribs with BBQ Sauce	57
Roasted Beef and Broccoli	53	Roasted Skirt Steaks	58
Lamb Curry Puffs	53	Beef Kebabs	58
Vegetable & Bacon Burgers	54	Herbed Rib-eye Steak	59
Roasted Leg of Lamb	54	Lemony Lamb Chops	59
Steak with Chimichurri Sauce	55	Short Beef Ribs	59
Homemade Korean Bulgogi	55	Simple Lamb Chops	60
Mongolian Beef	56	Fried Pork Chops	60

CHAPTER 7 DESSERTS RECIPES

Blueberry Pie	61	Apple Fritters	65
Typical Churros	61	Pumpkin Muffins	65
Vanilla Chocolate Cakes	62	Cinnamon Pears	65
Cinnamon Strawberry Crumble	62	Cinnamon Apricot Crisp	66
Caramelized Peaches	63	Pecan Brownies	66
Walnut Pie	63	Peanut Butter Cookies	66
Raisin Apple Dumplings	63	Chocolate Donuts	67
Cinnamon-Raisin Bread Pudding	64	Hazelnut Brownies	67
Apricot-Blueberry Crumble	64	Fluffy Orange Cake	67
Easy-to-Make Smores	64		

Conclusion **68**

Appendix 1 Measurement Conversion Chart **69**

Appendix 2 Recipes Index **70**

Introduction

Air fryers are becoming popular nowadays. People are looking for easy and quick options for almost everything in life. People are becoming conscious about their health and the way they look. This concern is moving the population to go for a healthier lifestyle as eating habits determine the weight and the diseases like cholesterol, cardiac issues, diabetes, etc. Air Fryers are dominating kitchens all over the world. The great thing about air fryers is that they are full of hot air. They are usually smaller in size similar to powerful ovens that use air as a vehicle for heat. Air fryers are much less messy than deep frying but give similar results without all the oil and fat required for deep frying.

The air fryer can cook all the foods that are cooked in ovens, microwaves, or deep frying. It can reheat the food without making the food rubbery. It is the perfect way to cook and prepare ingredients for a meal. Air fryers usually heat up in two to three minutes thus saving time, unlike conventional ovens which can usually take fifteen to twenty minutes. Air fryers offer a wide range of cooking functions depending on their model. It is a growing sensation for the healthy cooking option it provides.

The working principle of the air fryer resembles the countertop convection oven. The air fryer is an efficient way of prepping food with the conventional aspect of highly reduced prepping time as compared to traditional ovens and toasters. The air fryer functions due to the heating element which is strategically placed at the top of the device. A highly powerful fan takes that heat and transfers it to a basket which is placed inside the main unit. The fan ensures the rapid and smooth flow of air across the basket to cook the food properly. The hot air is evenly distributed across the food to make it crispy.

There is a general concept that air fryers are a healthier option than deep frying. But this is not the only advantage of the air fryer. There is a misconception of unhealthy pre-fried food like nuggets, chicken, fish sticks, French fries, etc. become healthier when they are cooked in the air fryer. However, cooking the food in an air fryer makes it only more crisp using the minimum oil as compared to the preparation of a similar item in the traditional oven.

What is the Breville Smart Air Fryer Oven?

Breville Smart Air Fryer Oven is popular for its function as a countertop oven that can air fry crispy French fires, roast for gatherings, and can dehydrate a wide variety of healthy foods. The cooking time can be reduced up to 30% due to super convection settings.

Benefits of Using Breville Smart Air Fryer Oven

The Breville Smart Air Fryer Oven offers many benefits. However, the most prominent benefits of this air fryer are stated as follows.

1. Chef in the Kitchen

The Breville Smart Air Fryer Oven provides a variety of functions like TOAST, BAGEL, BROIL, WARM, PROOF, REHEAT, AIR FRY/ DEHYDRATE, etc. The ability to perform all these functions makes the Breville Smart Air Fryer Oven not only an air fryer but a multi-cooker. This multi-cooker can prepare any required meal quickly for example air frying the snacks for the tea party to roasting the chicken for lunch.

2. Highly Versatile

The Breville Smart Air Fryer Oven is highly versatile with its LCD screen and buttons to control temperature, time, oven light, convection, phase cook, frozen foods, temperature conversion, and start/stop buttons. These buttons allow you to choose between different cooking functions. These buttons also allow controlling the time, temperature and convection before or during the cooking cycle.

3. Better Cooking Results

As compared to the traditional ovens and toasters, the Breville Smart Air Fryer Oven has given better cooking results. The food in this air fryer can be prepared in a delicious and extra juicy manner without increasing the calories of the food. Red meat along with turkey and chicken can be cooked in it hassle and mess-free.

4. Low Waiting Time

As the air fryer heats up quickly, the waiting time for cooking food and preheating the oven is considerably reduced in air fryers. Due to this reason, the frozen food can be placed in the oven and cooked to perfection without going to the trouble of defrosting and then cooking as required in the conventional ovens.

Main Functions of Breville Smart Air Fryer Oven

Food can be cooked at multiple racks at one time in Breville Smart Air Fryer Oven. While using the multiple racks, Rotate Remind feature should be used for the remainder of switching the position of food. This is necessary to get even and consistent results. Bake, roast, warm, proof, cookies, dehydrate, reheat, air fry, and pizza functions can use this Rotate Remind feature.

Following are some of the main functions of the Breville Smart Air Fryer Oven.

Toast Function

The function of toast is provided in the Breville Smart Air Fryer Oven. This is used for browning the bread from the outside to make it crispy on the outside and to keep it soft and moist from the inside. Different foods can be toasted in it but English muffins and frozen waffles are the ideal ones. Bread slices must be kept closer to the center of the wire rack for optimizing the toasting. The air fryer provides the options for the darkness settings. The darkness of the toast can be adjusted during or before the toasting cycle. The number of variables along with the temperature of the oven decides the cooking time. For this reason, even with the same color and slice settings, the cooking time may vary. This gives constant results.

Bagel Function

The bagel function is also available in the Breville air fryer. This function operates by lightly toasting the outside of the bagel while making the inside of the cut bagel crispy. There are thick-sliced pieces of bread that require one side to be toasted more than the other. This function is perfect for such cases along with toasting the crumpets. For optimum toasting, the bagel halves that have the cut side must

be placed as close to the center of the wire racks as possible. The darkness of the bagel and the number of halves of the bagel can be adjusted during the cycle. The heating elements must have the cut side of the bagel facing them to allow the bagel to get crisp from the cut side while the crust of the bagel remains lightly toasted.

Broil Function

The broil function is ideally used for cooking thin cuts of meat, poultry, fish, vegetables, sausages, and sandwiches. Browning, the top of dishes like gratins, desserts, casserole, etc. can be done by using the broiling function. For broiling, the food must be placed on the rack or in an oven-proof dish. The center of the wire rack must be placed such that the air flows around the food on all sides equally. The timing of broiling and its power level can be adjusted during or before the cycle.

Bake Function

The food is cooked thoroughly and evenly in the bake function. The Breville air fryer provides this function for baking cakes, brownies, muffins, pastries, etc. Prepackaged meals like lasagna and pot pies can be ideally cooked using the Bake function in the Breville air fryer. The rack position can be chosen depending upon the item being baked. The convection settings, baking time, and temperature can be adjusted during or before the cycle. When the bake function is started, the air fryer starts to preheat. After hearing the buzzer for the finishing of preheating food can be inserted into the oven. Food must be placed such that the air flows around it equally. The roasting pan is included in the air fryer. The roasting pan or any other oven-proof dish can be used in the oven.

Roast Function

The function of roast is also provided in the Breville Smart Air Fryer Oven. The function roast is used for cooking different types of meat and poultry. The roast function roasts the food to perfection from the outside while keeping it juicy and tender from the inside. Before or during the roasting cycle, the roasting temperature, time, and convection settings can be adjusted. The food should be placed in the oven such that the air flows equally around it. The temperature and time of the roasting cycle can be adjusted before or during the cycle.

Warm Function

The Breville air fryer also provides the Warm function. The Warm function is used to keep the food hot at the required temperature to reduce bacterial growth. The recommended temperature for this purpose is 160°F/70°C or above. The food is placed on a suitable rack such that the air flows equally around it. The temperature and convection settings can be done before or during the cycle.

Pizza Function

The pizza function is also available in the Breville Smart Air Fryer Oven. The pizza function is used to melt the cheese and brown the toppings. The crust of the pizza is also made crispy with this function. The temperature, time, convection and frozen settings of the pizza can be adjusted before or during the cycle. The time dial controls the maximum cooking time. The food should be placed at the center of the rack so that the air flows around all sides of the food. If the included pizza pan is being used, it should be placed in the oven during the preheated cycle for a better result. If the pizza stone is being used, it must be preheated without pizza to get optimized results.

Proof Function

The proof function is an important function and is provided in the Breville Smart Air Fryer Oven. The Proof function is used to precisely hold low temperatures which provides an ideal environment to proof the bread, pizza, rolls, and other dough. For this function, the wire rack must be placed in position 8. The time, temperature, and convection of proofing can be adjusted during the cycle.

Air Fry Function

The important function of the Breville Smart Air Fryer Oven is air frying. Air Frying is the combination of intense heat and maximum airflow to cook food. The air-fried food is crispy and brown. The air fry temperature, time, convection, and frozen settings can be adjusted before or during the cycle. The roasting must be used instead of an air fry/ dehydrate basket for cooking fatty foods (e.g. chicken wings) to prevent the dripping of oil. In between the batches, the excessive oil must be discarded. This oven can fit air frying/ dehydrating baskets. Additional baskets can be purchased online.

Reheat Function

The Reheat function available in the Breville Smart Air Fryer Oven is ideal for gently reheating the leftovers. This function reheats the leftovers without browning or drying them out. The food can be placed in the roasting pan, pizza pan, or other oven-proof dishes. The food must be placed at the center of the rack to allow the air to flow equally around the food. The temperature, time, convection, and frozen settings can be adjusted before or during the cycle.

Cookies Function

The Cookies function available in the Breville Smart Air Fryer Oven is ideally used for baking homemade or commercially prepared cookies. Other baked treats can also be made using this function. The Cookies temperature, time, convection, and frozen settings can be adjusted before or during the cycle.

Slow Cook Function

This provided function allows cooking profiles that are designed for long times at low temperatures. The slow cook temperature, time, and convection settings can be adjusted before or during the cycle. The cookware must not be pulled further than halfway out when inserting or removing cookware from the oven. Heavy cookware should not be allowed to rest on the glass when the door is open.

Dehydrate Function

The dehydrate function provided in the Breville Smart Air Fryer

Oven is used to combine low and stable heat with maximized airflow to evenly dry out foods without cooking or overheating. Food must be spread evenly on the included air-fry/ dehydrate basket into the rack position. Food must be placed in a single layer and space must be left between the pieces to get the best results. The dehydrating temperature, time, and convection settings can be adjusted before or

during the cycle. For foods with strong colors, baking paper can be used on air-fry/ dehydrate basket to prevent staining. A roasting pan can be used to catch the drippings from the dehydrating foods.

Phase Cook

The phase cook button available in the Breville Smart Air Fryer Oven is used to program 2 back to back cooking functions. The functions available for the Phase cook are broil, bake, roast, warm, and pizza. After the completion of the first cooking phase, the second one automatically starts.

Components of Breville Air Fryer Oven

The following are the main components of Breville Air Fryer.

1. Main Unit

The main body of the air fryer is made from high-quality stainless steel. The main unit can be cleaned by using a sponge or damp cloth. The main unit must not be inserted in any liquid including water.

2. Door Handle

This part remains cold during the cooking process. This handle must always be used while handling the food in the oven instead of the glass door.

3. LCD Display Panel

The LCD provides the interface for the selection, adjustment, swift programming, or monitoring of cooking functions. The color of the light of the LCD changes according to the cooking function active.

4. Glass Door

This part is made from high-quality glass which keeps the heat inside and ensures the even distribution of heat across the food.

5. Control Panel

The control panel of the air fryer contains control knobs for time and temperature and cooking functions.

6. Pizza Pan

The Pizza pan is used for toasting pizzas, bread, and bagels. The 13-inch non-stick pizza pan could also be used for other functions like roasting, grilling, and baking.

7. Wire Rack

The wire rack is reversible for 8 different rack positions and it is used

to place food in the oven. Two wire racks come with this air fryer.

8. Broiling Rack

The broiling rack is used to place the food while using the broil function. It is a 9x13 inches rack.

9. Roasting Pan

This pan is used to place the food in it while roasting. It can also be used as a dripping tray for fatty foods during dehydration.

10. Air Fry/ Dehydrate Basket

This tray is used to place the food while dehydrating or air frying. The food is placed on it with spaces or at a distance.

Other accessories included in this air fryer are oven light, ventilation slots, crumb tray, Breville Assist pug, SELECT/CONFIRM dial, and ROTATE REMIND button. The air fryer contains different buttons like TEMPERATURE dial/toast and bagel darkness control, TIME dial/toast and bagel slice selection, START/STOP button, OVEN LIGHT button, CONVECTION button, PHASE COOK button, FROZEN FOODS button, TEMPERATURE CONVERSION button, and volume adjustment button.

Before First Using Instructions

Preparing the Oven

It is required to run the oven empty for 20 minutes in order to remove the protective substances on the heating elements. The area must be properly ventilated as the oven might emit vapors that are safe and do not reduce the performance of the oven.

1. The first step will be removing the packing material, promotional labels, and tape from the oven and discarding them.

2. After that remove all the trays of the oven like crumb trays, wire racks, broiling rack, roasting pan, air fry/dehydrate basket, and pizza pans from the polyfoam packaging. These trays should be washed with a soft sponge in soapy water and then dried thoroughly.

3. The next step is wiping the interior of the oven with a soft damp sponge. Dry it thoroughly.

4. Find a dry flat surface and place the oven on it. There must be a minimum distance of 4 inches on both sides of the oven and a 6 inches

distance on the upper side.

5. Take the crumb tray and insert it into the oven.

6. After unwinding the power cord completely, insert the power plug into the grounded power outlet.

7. The oven will produce an alert sound and illuminate the LCD screen. The function options will appear on the screen with the indicator pointing towards the TOAST setting by default.

8. Using the SELECT/CONFIRM dial, move the indicator to the PIZZA function.

9. Now pressing the START/STOP button will illuminate red, the LCD screen will illuminate orange and the oven alert will sound.

10. The LCD screen will give blinking PREHEATING. After the completion of preheating, the oven will give an alert.

11. The timer will begin to display and automatically start a

countdown.

12. When the cooking cycles are complete, the oven will give an alert sound. The light of the START/STOP button will go out and the LCD screen will become white.

13. The oven is now ready to use.

Care and Cleaning

The cleaning of the oven requires that the oven must be turned off. This is done by removing the power plug from the power outlet. Before cleaning and disassembling the oven and all of its accessories must be completely cooled.

Cleaning the outer body and door

1. Using a damp and soft sponge or cloth, clean the outer body of the oven. To avoid the build-up of stains, a mild and non-abrasive cleanser or spray can be used. The cleanser should be applied to the cloth first. It must not be directly applied to the oven surface.

2. Using a soft plastic scouring pad or damp sponge, clean the glass door using a mild detergent or glass cleaner. To avoid scratching on the glass door do not use the abrasive cleanser or metal scouring pad.

3. Clean the LCD using a soft sponge or cloth with a cleanser. Do not use cleanser directly on the LCD or the dry cloth. They will scratch the surface of the LCD.

4. Before turning the oven on, let all the surfaces dry thoroughly. After that insert the power plug into a power outlet.

Immersing the body, power cord, or power plug in water or any other liquid will cause electrocution. It must be avoided at all costs.

Cleaning the interior

The interior walls of the oven are made from a non-stick coating making the cleaning of the oven easy. Wiping the walls with a soft damp sponge will clean all the splattering that might happen during the cooking. To avoid the build-up of stains, use the non-abrasive cleanser. The cleanser must be applied to the sponge first. It must never be applied directly to the surface. Touching the quartz heating elements must be avoided. Extreme caution must be taken while cleaning the quartz heating element. Allow the oven to be completely cooled and then clean along the length of the heating element using a

cloth. No cleaning agent should be used. Before inserting the power plug and turning on the oven, let all the surfaces dry completely.

Cleaning the crumb tray

1. The crumb tray must be cleaned after every use by sliding it out and wiping it with a soft, damp cloth or sponge using a non-abrasive cleanser. The tray must be dried thoroughly before inserting it again.

2. Baked-on grease on the crumb tray can be removed by soaking the tray in soapy water and then washing it with a soft plastic scouring pad or soft sponge. Properly rinse and dry the tray.

3. The crumb tray must always be inserted into the oven before inserting the power plug into the power outlet and turning on the oven. Cleaning the wire rack, broiling rack, roasting pan, and pizza pan

1. Using a plastic scouring pad or soft sponge, wash all these accessories in warm soapy water. Thoroughly dry and rinse. Avoid the use of abrasive cleansers and metal scouring pads to clean any of the accessories. These things damage the surface of the accessories.

2. These accessories should not be placed in the dishwasher to extend their life.

Storage

1. Remove the plug from the power outlet and turn off the oven.

2. Before disassembling and cleaning, allow all the oven accessories to cool completely.

3. All accessories and ovens must be clean and dry.

4. Insert the broiling rack in the roasting pan and rest it on the wire rack in the middle rack height position and insert the crumb tray. Ensure that all these steps are done.

5. Close the door.

6. The device must be stored in the upright position on its support legs. Do not put anything on the top of the oven.

Troubleshooting

To use the device properly, the following troubleshooting approaches

should be used.

1. The oven will not switch "ON"

The reason for this may be that the power cable is not properly inserted or the power outlet is faulty. It can be solved by checking that the power plug is inserted properly into the outlet. Or by inserting the power plug into the independent or different outlet. If it still does not switch on, try resetting the circuit breaker.

2. I would like to have the default LCD settings back

The oven is designed to remember the last setting used for each function. It will remember the last setting even when the plug is removed from the outlet. To restore the default settings of the oven, the user is required to press and hold for five seconds the

TEMPERATURE CONVERSION and FROZEN buttons.

3. The LCD light has gone out

This happens because if the oven is not used for ten minutes it goes into standby mode. The LCD screen ceases to illuminate during the standby mode. Although the LCD light goes out, all the function options are still visible.

To get the oven out of standby mode, turn any dial or press the

START/STOP button. This will cause the LCD to re-illuminate.

4. The pizza does not cook evenly

This occurs because large pizzas require to be rotated halfway through the cooking. To counter this problem, open the door of the oven halfway through the cooking and rotate the pizza to 180 degrees. This will give more even darkness to the pizza. ROTATE REMIND should also be used.

5. The magnetic Auto-Rack Eject comes out too far when I open the door

This issue can be resolved by opening the rack slowly. The controlled opening of the rack when it is placed in the 3 or 4 positions of the rack will prevent the rack from ejecting too quickly.

6. I cannot select the frozen foods button

The frozen food button is not selectable for every function provided in the air fryer. It can only be selected for the following functions: TOAST, BAGEL, PIZZA, AIRFRY, REHEAT and COOKIES.

7. Steam is coming out from the oven door

The steam coming out of the oven door is normal. This is because the door is vented to release the steam. High moisture contents food like frozen pieces of bread can release too much steam which is vented out through the door.

8. The heating elements appear to be pulsing

The heat inside the oven is controlled by the Element IQ. It controls the heat by pulsing the power and adjusting the power level in the heating element. It does this in short bursts to accurately control the temperature. This is normal for the oven.

9. Water is dripping onto the counter from under the door

The high moisture content foods like frozen loaves of bread drip the water inside of the door onto the counter. This happens because of condensation. This phenomenon is normal.

10. The temperature reading on the LCD does not match the temperature measured inside the oven

To make the measurements standard, the TOAST position has been used to calibrate the temperatures. This has been done with the center of the middle rack without having any tray inserted. In this position, re-check the temperature. The door must not be opened for thirty minutes as this will cause the heat to escape every time the door is opened. At 75% of the target temperature, the preheat alert sounds.

11. The Preheat alert sounds at a lower temperature than what is

displayed on the screen

To provide the fastest, combined cooking and preheating time, the preheat alert of the oven sounds at 75% of the targeted temperature.

The opening of the door by the user to insert the food into the oven causes significant heat loss inside the oven. The preheating sound alerts the user at 75% of the targeted value. if this happened at 100% of the targeted temperature, the opening of the door will result in a significant loss of heat and a waste of waiting time. By sounding the alert at 75% of the temperature, opening the door to place the food inside the oven will recover the temperature up to 2 minutes faster. For this reason, the temperature on the LCD screen and the targeted temperature do not match at the time of preheating alert. The oven can take up to 8-10 minutes to start and to reach the target temperature including the opening of the oven door when the preheat alert sounds.

12. The LCD screen displays "E01"

This error occurs when there is a non-resettable error. When this error is displayed on the screen, immediately remove the power cable from the power outlet and call Breville consumer Support.

13. The LCD screen displays "E02"

When there is a non-resettable issue with the appliance this error usually occurs. When this error appears on the LCD of the machine, instantly remove the power cable from the power outlet and call Consumer support at Breville.

14. The LCD screen displays "E03"

This error occurs on the LCD screen when the temperature is set above the maximum limit. To counter this error, remove the plug from the outlet. Allow the oven to properly cool for around 15 minutes and then when it cools down plug it back in. If this message continues to appear on the screen, call Consumer support at Breville.

15. The LCD screen displays "E06"

The error E06 appears on the LCD screen of the oven when there is a non-resettable issue with the appliance. When this error occurs, immediately remove the power cable from the power outlet and call

Consumer support at Breville.

16. The Temperature are changing when the convection button is pressed

To increase the cooking rate, compensation for the convection fan is required. This is done by calibrating the temperature and it results in the changing temperatures when the convection button is pressed. This is a normal case.

17. Noise from the control panel

The noise from the oven is due to the fan acting as the heat sink. When the temperature of the oven increases above 302°F/ 150°C, the electronicss cooling fan in the appliance is turned on. But when the temperature goes below 302°F/150°C the fan turns off automatically and the noise will be gone.

4-Week Diet Plan

Week 1

Day 1:

Breakfast: Homemade Cheese & Sausage Burritos
Lunch: Cheese Tomato Halves
Snack: Roasted Chickpeas
Dinner: Mini Beef Burger
Dessert: Hazelnut Brownies

Day 2:

Breakfast: Baby Spinach Frittata
Lunch: Cheese Broccoli Casserole
Snack: Breaded Avocado Fries
Dinner: Spicy Chicken Wings
Dessert: Peanut Butter Cookies

Day 3:

Breakfast: Buttermilk Biscuits
Lunch: Brussels Sprouts
Snack: Chicken Tenders
Dinner: Flavorful Tilapia Fillets
Dessert: Cinnamon Apricot Crisp

Day 4:

Breakfast: Oatmeal Porridge with Strawberries
Lunch: Herbed Head Cauliflower
Snack: Mac & Cheese Balls
Dinner: Chicken Pot Pie
Dessert: Pumpkin Muffins

Day 5:

Breakfast: Cheese Sausage Pizza
Lunch: Tasty Falafels with Tahini Sauce
Snack: Exotic Chicken Meatballs
Dinner: Crab Shrimp Roll
Dessert: Easy-to-Make Smores

Day 6:

Breakfast: Ham Omelet
Lunch: Parmesan Eggplant
Snack: Breaded Zucchini Sticks
Dinner: Ribeye Steak
Dessert: Cinnamon-Raisin Bread Pudding

Day 7:

Breakfast: Baked Rolls
Lunch: Spicy Okra Fries
Snack: Bacon Wrapped Avocado
Dinner: Herb Chicken Thighs
Dessert: Fluffy Orange Cake

Week 2

Day 1:

Breakfast: Egg Toast Cups
Lunch: Pumpkin Pieces
Snack: Baked Crackers
Dinner: Sirloin Steaks
Dessert: Walnut Pie

Day 2:

Breakfast: Potato Pancakes
Lunch: Golden Crispy Onion Rings
Snack: Ravioli
Dinner: Broiled Lobster Tail
Dessert: Vanilla Chocolate Cakes

Day 3:

Breakfast: Cheese-Bacon Stuffed Bell Peppers
Lunch: Stuffed Mushrooms
Snack: Homemade Potato Chips
Dinner: Turkey Thighs
Dessert: Blueberry Pie

Day 4:

Breakfast: Simple Banana Bread
Lunch: Breaded Cauliflower Fritters
Snack: Spinach Rolls
Dinner: Cajun Salmon Fillet
Dessert: Chocolate Donuts

Day 5:

Breakfast: Banana Bread Pudding
Lunch: Carrots & Turnips
Snack: Tasty Cheese Sticks
Dinner: Chicken Breasts
Dessert: Pecan Brownies

Day 6:

Breakfast: Vanilla Cinnamon Granola
Lunch: Acorn Squash Slices
Snack: Sweet Potato Chips
Dinner: Mongolian Beef
Dessert: Cinnamon Pears

Day 7:

Breakfast: Potato Protein Burrito
Lunch: Fried Tofu Cubes
Snack: Broiled Corn
Dinner: Fried Crusted Chicken
Dessert: Apple Fritters

Week 3

Day 1:

Breakfast: Cheese Sausage Frittata
Lunch: Cheese Balls
Snack: Tasty Cauliflower Fritters
Dinner: Glazed Salmon Fillets
Dessert: Apricot-Blueberry Crumble

Day 2:

Breakfast: Baked Potatoes & Bell Peppers
Lunch: Green Beans and Mushrooms
Snack: Simple French Fries
Dinner: Herbed Turkey Breast
Dessert: Raisin Apple Dumplings

Day 3:

Breakfast: Feta Shakshuka
Lunch: Onion Cauliflower Tacos
Snack: Baked Pumpkin Seeds
Dinner: Fried Pork Chops
Dessert: Cinnamon Strawberry Crumble

Day 4:

Breakfast: Saucy Salmon Fillets
Lunch: Fried Tofu Bites
Snack: Jicama Strips
Dinner: Roasted Chicken Thighs
Dessert: Caramelized Peaches

Day 5:

Breakfast: Egg Rolls
Lunch: Onion & Sweet Potato Hash
Snack: Easy Plantain Pieces
Dinner: Cod Fillets
Dessert: Typical Churros

Day 6:

Breakfast: Air Fried Potato Pieces
Lunch: Delicious Cauliflower in Buffalo Sauce
Snack: Stuffed Red Potatoes
Dinner: Simple Lamb Chops
Dessert: Hazelnut Brownies

Day 7:

Breakfast: Zucchini-Apple Bread
Lunch: Parmesan Brussels Sprout
Snack: Mini Sausage Pizzas
Dinner: Herbed Turkey Roast
Dessert: Cinnamon Apricot

Week 4

Day 1:

Breakfast: Cream Spinach Pie
Lunch: Broccoli Gratin
Snack: Crispy Chickpeas
Dinner: Roasted Round Beef
Dessert: Easy-to-Make Smores

Day 2:

Breakfast: Banana Bread Pudding
Lunch: Cheese Balls
Snack: Roasted Chickpeas
Dinner: Dijon Tuna Cakes
Dessert: Raisin Apple Dumplings

Day 3:

Breakfast: Baby Spinach Frittata
Lunch: Cheese Broccoli Casserole
Snack: Mac & Cheese Balls
Dinner: Crispy Spiced Chicken
Dessert: Walnut Pie

Day 4:

Breakfast: Buttermilk Biscuits
Lunch: Herbed Head Cauliflower
Snack: Breaded Zucchini Sticks
Dinner: Lamb Curry Puffs
Dessert: Chocolate Donuts

Day 5:

Breakfast: Baked Potatoes & Bell Peppers
Lunch: Tasty Falafels with Tahini Sauce
Snack: Homemade Potato Chips
Dinner: Popcorn Chicken
Dessert: Blueberry Pie

Day 6:

Breakfast: Ham Omelet
Lunch: Pumpkin Pieces
Snack: Broiled Corn
Dinner: Roasted Leg of Lamb
Dessert: Vanilla Chocolate Cakes

Day 7:

Breakfast: Air Fried Potato Pieces
Lunch: Stuffed Mushrooms
Snack: Jicama Strips
Dinner: Dijon Turkey Breast
Dessert: Cinnamon Apricot Crisp

Egg Toast Cups

Prep Time: 5 minutes | Cook Time: 15 minutes | Serves: 4

1 non-stick cooking spray
4 slice whole-wheat bread (toasted)
1 ½ tablespoons trans-fat free tub margarine (such as I Can't Believe It's Not

Butter)
1 slice (about 2 ounces) deli-style ham, sliced into ½-inch strips
4 large eggs
⅛ teaspoon salt
⅛ teaspoon black pepper

1. Select the BAKE function, and adjust the temperature at 375°F/190°C and set the time for 13 minutes. 2. Press the START/STOP button to activate the function, and allow it to preheat. 3. Prepare 4 (8-ounce) oven-safe custard cups or ramekins and spritz the inside with non-stick cooking spray. 4. Spread the margarine over one side of the bread and then arrange it inside a ramekin, margarine-side down. Gently press inside the cup. Repeat for the rest three. 5. Add the ham strips to the cups in a single layer and crack one egg into each cup. Add salt and pepper to season. 6. Arrange the custard cups in the roasting pan and insert them inside the preheated oven on position 6. 7. When the egg cups are done, carefully remove them from the oven and transfer the cups to a serving plate.
Per Serving: Calories 139; Fat 5.66g; Sodium 294mg; Carbs 16.47g; Fiber 2.1g; Sugar 0.33g; Protein 6.44g

Ham Omelet

Prep Time: 10 minutes | Cook Time: 7 minutes | Serves: 2

4 large eggs
3½ ounces ham, cut into small pieces
¼ cup milk
¾ cup mixed vegetables (white mushrooms, green onions, red pepper)
¼ cup mixed cheddar and mozzarella

cheese
1 teaspoon freshly chopped mixed herbs (cilantro and chives)
Salt and freshly ground pepper to taste

1. Turn the SELECT/CONFIRM dial until the indicator on the LCD screen reaches the BAKE function, turn the TEMPERATURE dial to adjust the temperature to 350ºF/175ºC, and then turn the TIME dial to adjust the time to 7 minutes. 2. Press the START/STOP button to activate the function, and allow it to preheat. 3. Beat the eggs with milk in a mixing bowl, then add ham, mixed vegetables, salt, and ground pepper, and beat them together. 4. Grease the pizza pan with olive oil, and then pour the egg mixture into it. 5. Once preheated, insert the pan inside the oven on position 6, and then bake the omelet for 5 to 7 minutes. 6. Top the omelet with the remaining cheese and mixed herbs halfway through cooking. 7. When done, serve warm.
Per Serving: Calories 287; Fat 15.54g; Sodium 865mg; Carbs 11.15g; Fiber 0.5g; Sugar 4.31g; Protein 25.13g

Broiled Corn

Prep Time: 5 minutes | Cook Time: 10 minutes | Serves: 4

4 fresh ears of corn
2 to 3 teaspoons Vegetable

oil
Salt and pepper to taste

1. Remove the husk of the corn. Wash them and pat them dry. 2. Brush the corn with vegetable oil and add salt and pepper to season, and then place them in the broiling rack.3. Insert the rack inside the oven on position 2, and then broil the food at High for 10 minutes.4. When the cooking time is up, carefully remove the rack from the oven. 5. Serve and enjoy!
Per Serving: Calories 147; Fat 3.98g; Sodium 22mg; Carbs 28.26g; Fiber 4g; Sugar 5.18g; Protein 4.83g

Oatmeal Porridge with Strawberries

Prep Time: 10 minutes | Cook Time: 10 minutes | Serves: 2

2 cups strawberries, sliced and divided
1 cup milk
1 cup rolled oats
4 tablespoons brown sugar
½ teaspoon ground cinnamon

½ teaspoon baking powder
4 tablespoons almonds, slivered
Pinch of salt

1. Reserve 1 cup of strawberries. Combine the remaining ingredients well in an oven-proof bowl. Then allow it to sit for 10 minutes. 2. Sprinkle the reserved strawberries on top, and then place the bowl in the roasting pan. 3. Turn the SELECT/CONFIRM dial until the indicator on the LCD screen reaches the BAKE function, turn the TEMPERATURE dial to adjust the temperature to 350ºF/175ºC, and then turn the TIME dial to adjust the time to 10 minutes. 4. Press the START/STOP button to activate the function, and allow it to preheat. 5. Once preheated, insert the pan inside the oven on position 6, and let the porridge bake. 6. When cooked, carefully remove the bowl from the oven. 7. Serve and enjoy!
Per Serving: Calories 315; Fat 8.94g; Sodium 135mg; Carbs 65.6g; Fiber 10.8g; Sugar 29.65g; Protein 13.47g

Cheese-Bacon Stuffed Bell Peppers

Prep Time: 10 minutes | Cook Time: 15 minutes | Serves: 4

8 eggs
4 bell peppers cut the top & remove seeds
1 cup Parmesan cheese, grated

¼ onion, chopped
3 ounces bacon, cooked & chopped
Pepper
Salt

1. Select the BAKE function, and adjust the temperature at 390°F/200°C and set the time for 15 minutes. 2. Press the START/STOP button to activate the function, and allow the oven to preheat. 3. Add the chopped onion and bacon to the hollow bell peppers. 4. For each bell pepper, crack 2 eggs in and add ¼ cup grated Parmesan cheese on top. Add salt and pepper to season. 5. Arrange the stuffed bell peppers inside the roasting pan and insert them inside the oven on position 6. 6. When the cooking time is up, carefully remove the pan from the oven. 7. Serve and enjoy!
Per Serving: Calories 302; Fat 20.58g; Sodium 913mg; Carbs 10.64g; Fiber 1.5g; Sugar 2.89g; Protein 19.96g

Cream Spinach Pie

Prep Time: 10 minutes | Cook Time: 20 minutes | Serves: 4

5 eggs
10 ounces frozen spinach, squeezed & drained
¼ cup heavy cream
1 cup Cheddar cheese, shredded

¼ teaspoon garlic powder
¼ cup onion, diced
Pepper
Salt

1. Select the BAKE function, and adjust the temperature at 320°F/160°C and set the time for 20 minutes. 2. Press the START/STOP button to activate the function, and allow the oven to preheat. 3. Whisk the heavy cream, pepper, salt, garlic powder, and eggs in a bowl, then stir in cheese, onion, and spinach. 4. Prepare a suitable baking dish and lightly grease it with olive oil. Place the baking dish on the wire rack. 5. Insert the rack together with the baking dish in the oven on position 6, and then bake the pie. 6. When the cooking time is up, carefully remove the rack from the oven. 7. Serve and enjoy!
Per Serving: Calories 230; Fat 13.47g; Sodium 798mg; Carbs 10.85g; Fiber 2.3g; Sugar 5.19g; Protein 17.41g

Cheese Sausage Pizza

Prep Time: 5 minutes | Cook Time: 15minutes | Serves: 4

Crescent dough
3 eggs, scrambled
Crumbled sausage

½ chopped pepper
½ cup Cheddar cheese
½ cup Mozzarella cheese

1. Spray the pizza pan over with cooking oil, and then evenly arrange the dough on the pan. 2. Turn the SELECT/CONFIRM dial until the indicator on the LCD screen reaches the PIZZA function, turn the TEMPERATURE dial to adjust the temperature to 350ºF/175ºC, and then turn the TIME dial to adjust the time to 10 minutes. 3. Press the START/STOP button to activate the function, and allow it to preheat. 4. Once preheated, insert the pan inside the oven on position 7, and then cook the pizza for 5 to 10 minutes. 5. When cooked, carefully remove the pan from the oven. 6. Serve and enjoy!
Per Serving: Calories 202; Fat 11.33g; Sodium 580mg; Carbs 8.02g; Fiber 0.6g; Sugar 2.99g; Protein 16.77g

Baked Potatoes & Bell Peppers

Prep Time: 15 minutes | Cook Time: 50 minutes | Serves: 4

2 pounds red potatoes, sliced into even, ¾″ pieces
1 red bell pepper
½ medium white onion

2 tablespoons extra-virgin olive oil
1 teaspoon garlic powder
½ teaspoon sea salt
Ground black pepper

1. Turn the SELECT/CONFIRM dial until the indicator on the LCD screen reaches the BAKE function, turn the TEMPERATURE dial to adjust the temperature to 425ºF/220ºC, and then turn the TIME dial to adjust the time to 50 minutes. 2. Press the START/STOP button to activate the function, and allow it to preheat. 3. Add onion, bell pepper, and the potatoes to the roasting pan, and then add 2 tablespoons oil, salt, ground black pepper, and garlic powder to season. 4. Toss them to coat well and arrange them in an even layer on the pan. 5. Once preheated, insert the pan inside the oven on position 6, and then bake the food for 45 to 50 minutes. 6. When cooked, carefully remove the pan from the oven. 7. Serve and enjoy!
Per Serving: Calories 200; Fat 3.41g; Sodium 394mg; Carbs 39.27g; Fiber 4.5g; Sugar 4.13g; Protein 4.86g

Egg Rolls

Prep Time: 10 minutes | Cook Time: 10 minutes | Serves: 4

4 eggs
Pinch of salt
Pinch of pepper
1 teaspoon butter
½ cup Cheddar cheese shredded

4 slices bacon cooked and crumbled
4 egg roll wrappers

1. Turn the SELECT/CONFIRM dial until the indicator on the LCD screen reaches the AIRFRY function, turn the TEMPERATURE dial to adjust the temperature to 390ºF/200ºC, and then turn the TIME dial to adjust the time to 8 minutes. 2. Press the START/STOP button to activate the function, and allow it to preheat. 3. Crack the eggs in a small mixing bowl and add salt and pepper to season. Whisk well to combine. 4. In a skillet, add the butter and heat over medium heat until melted. 5. Top with Cheddar cheese and bacon crumbles and whisk until well incorporated. 6. Lightly brush the edges of the egg rolls with water. Place ¼ of the egg mixture on the centre of the egg rolls. Fold in the left edge with the right edge, and then fold the bottom corner up. Roll the egg roll and seal the top point with more water, as needed. 7. Repeat with the remaining rolls. 8. Arrange the egg rolls evenly in the roasting pan and insert them inside the preheated oven on position 3. 9. Cook them for 8 minutes, flipping halfway through cooking. 10. Carefully remove the pan from the oven. 11. Serve and enjoy!
Per Serving: Calories 391; Fat 23.82g; Sodium 767mg; Carbs 23.86g; Fiber 0.7g; Sugar 3.44g; Protein 19.4g

Vanilla Cinnamon Granola

Prep Time: 10 minutes | Cook Time: 20 minutes | Serves: 4

1½ cups rolled oats
¼ cup maple syrup
¼ cup pecan pieces

1 teaspoon vanilla extract
½ teaspoon ground cinnamon

1. Line the roasting pan with parchment paper. 2. Mix the oats, maple syrup, cinnamon, vanilla, and pecan pieces in a large bowl to coat the oats and the pecan pieces thoroughly. 3. Evenly spread the mixture in the roasting pan. 4. Turn the SELECT/CONFIRM dial until the indicator on the LCD screen reaches the BAKE function, turn the TEMPERATURE dial to adjust the temperature to 300ºF/150ºC, and then turn the TIME dial to adjust the time to 20 minutes. 5. Press the START/STOP button to activate the function, and allow it to preheat. 6. Once preheated, insert the roasting pan inside the oven on position 6, and then bake the dish for 20 minutes, stirring once halfway through cooking. 7. When cooked, carefully remove the pan from the oven. Allow the dish to sit to cool for about 30 minutes before serving.
Per Serving: Calories 185; Fat 6.96g; Sodium 4mg; Carbs 37.8g; Fiber 6.2g; Sugar 12.81g; Protein 6.69g

Baby Spinach Frittata

Prep Time: 10 minutes | Cook Time: 35 minutes | Serves: 6

12 eggs
½ cup cheddar cheese, grated
1 ½ cups cherry tomatoes, cut in half
½ cup fresh basil, chopped

1 cup baby spinach, chopped
½ cup yogurt
Salt and pepper to taste

1. Beat the eggs with yogurt in a bowl.2. Spritz the roasting pan with cooking spray or cooking oil; layer the spinach, basil, tomatoes, and cheese in the pan, and then top them with the egg mixture. 3. Turn the SELECT/CONFIRM dial until the indicator on the LCD screen reaches the BAKE function, turn the TEMPERATURE dial to adjust the temperature to 390ºF/200ºC, and then turn the TIME dial to adjust the time to 35 minutes.4. Press the START/STOP button to activate the function, and allow it to preheat. 5. Once preheated, insert the roasting pan inside the oven on position 6, and then bake the food for 35 minutes.6. Serve warm.
Per Serving: Calories 175; Fat 10.76g; Sodium 347mg; Carbs 4.42g; Fiber 0.3g; Sugar 2.9g; Protein 14.56g

Cheese Sausage Frittata

Prep Time: 15 minutes | Cook Time: 20 minutes | Serves: 2

¼ pound breakfast sausage
4 lightly beaten eggs
½ cup shredded Cheddar cheese

2 tablespoons diced red bell pepper
1 chopped green onion
Cooking spray
1 pinch cayenne pepper (optional)

1. Mix eggs, sausage, cheddar, Cayenne, green onion, and the chopped red bell pepper in a bowl; transfer the mixture to the pizza pan or roasting pan. 2. Turn the SELECT/CONFIRM dial until the indicator on the LCD screen reaches the AIRFRY function, turn the TEMPERATURE dial to adjust the temperature to 360ºF/180ºC, and then turn the TIME dial to adjust the time to 20 minutes. 3. Press the START/STOP button to activate the function, and allow it to preheat. 4. Once preheated, insert the pan inside the oven on position 3, and then let the food air fry for 18 to 20 minutes. 5. Serve and enjoy!
Per Serving: Calories 415; Fat 23.82g; Sodium 1126mg; Carbs 20.65g; Fiber 1.7g; Sugar 13.03g; Protein 28.82g

Potato Protein Burrito

Prep Time: 20 minutes | Cook Time: 20 minutes | Serves: 10

Tortillas
14 ounces ground sausage
Second protein (ham, ground chicken, bacon)
2 cups chopped potatoes
½ cup red onion
½ cup diced bell peppers, red, green, and yellow
6-8 eggs
½ teaspoon salt
1 teaspoon pepper
½ teaspoon garlic powder
1 teaspoon Italian seasoning
2 cups shredded cheese
2 tablespoons butter
3 tablespoons olive oil

1. Heat 2 tablespoons of butter and 3 tablespoons of olive oil in the pan or skillet over medium heat; add the potatoes and cook them for 7 to 8 minutes; add the onion and peppers, and cook them for 3 to 4 minutes. Transfer them to a plate and set aside for later use. 2. Add the proteins to the same pan or skillet, and cook. Drain and remove from the pan. 3. Scramble the eggs in the same pan or skillet and lightly season them with salt and pepper. 4. In the center of the tortilla, add scrambled eggs with a spoon and lightly mash down to hold the remaining ingredients, then add the proteins, potatoes, and veggies, and then sprinkle the cheese on top. Tightly roll the burrito. 5. Place the burrito on the roasting pan. 6. Turn the SELECT/CONFIRM dial until the indicator on the LCD screen reaches the BAKE function, turn the TEMPERATURE dial to adjust the temperature to 360ºF/180ºC, and then turn the TIME dial to adjust the time to 6 minutes. 7. Press the START/STOP button to activate the function, and allow it to preheat. 8. Once preheated, insert the roasting pan inside the oven on position 6, and let the machine work. 9. Serve warm.

Per Serving: Calories 354; Fat 24.69g; Sodium 462mg; Carbs 10.56g; Fiber 1.1g; Sugar 1.73g; Protein 22.27g

Baked Rolls

Prep Time: 30 minutes | Cook Time: 20 minutes | Serves: 6

For The Dough:
¾ cup warm milk, 100-110°F
2 ¼ teaspoons active yeast
¼ cup granulated sugar
1 egg + 1 egg yolk, room temperature
¼ cup unsalted butter, melted
3 cups all-purpose flour and more for dusting
¾ teaspoon salt

For The Filling:
⅔ cup light brown sugar
1 ½ tablespoons ground cinnamon
¼ cup unsalted butter, room temperature

For The Cream Cheese Frosting:
4 ounces cream cheese, room temperature
4 tablespoons unsalted butter, room temperature
¾ cup powdered sugar
1 teaspoon vanilla extract

1. Pour lukewarm milk into a bowl and add the active yeast, stir well and allow it to sit for 5 minutes. 2. Add sugar, melted butter, and eggs and combine well. Add salt and the all-purpose flour to the mixture when the dough is about to be formed. 3. Mix the dough into a ball with a stand mixer on medium and add flour as needed to avoid the ball from sticking to the bowl. 4. Transfer the dough into a greased bowl and cover with plastic wrap and a hot towel. Let it sit on a clean work surface for about 1 hour 30 minutes or until the dough has doubled the size. 5. Turn the SELECT/CONFIRM dial until the indicator on the LCD screen reaches the BAKE function, turn the TEMPERATURE dial to adjust the temperature to 350ºF/175ºC, and then turn the TIME dial to adjust the time to 15 minutes. 6. Press the START/STOP button to activate the function, and allow it to preheat. 7. Portion the dough into two. Then flatten them into one square meter with a rolling pin on a lightly floured surface. 8. Lightly rub the dough with butter and leave a small edge. 9. In a small bowl, add sugar and cinnamon and mix well. Then sprinkle over the buttered dough. Lightly press the dough. 10. Cut the flattened dough into 1 ½-inch wide strips with a pizza cutter. Then roll the strips. 11. Arrange the cinnamon rolls evenly in the roasting pan and insert them in the preheated oven on Position 6. Bake them for 15 minutes, and you can work in batches. 12. While baking, add the frosting ingredients to a medium bowl and beat together until smooth. 13. Carefully remove the pan from the oven after baking. 14. Sprinkle the frosting on top and serve.

Per Serving: Calories 537; Fat 23.51g; Sodium 409mg; Carbs 70.46g; Fiber 3.1g; Sugar 19.31g; Protein 11.16g

Feta Shakshuka

Prep Time: 5 minutes | Cook Time: 25 minutes | Serves: 6

1¼ cup chopped parsley	1 red pepper
½ cup chopped mint	3 garlic cloves
½ cup chopped tarragon	1 teaspoon cumin
¼ cup chopped capers	1 teaspoon smoked paprika
1 tablespoon chopped anchovies	1 teaspoon turmeric
2 teaspoons Dijon mustard	2 cans (14-oz) chopped tomatoes
⅓ cup extra-virgin olive oil	⅔ cup crumbled Feta
1 red onion	6 eggs

1. Mix the parsley, mint, anchovies, and tarragon in a bowl; add oil and mustard to the mixture, and then set them aside for later use. 2. Cook the onion, peppers, and garlic in the skillet for 10 minutes; add the tomatoes and spices to them, and simmer for 5 minutes; add the feta, and mustard mixture, then transfer them to roasting pan. 3. Turn the SELECT/CONFIRM dial until the indicator on the LCD screen reaches the BAKE function, turn the TEMPERATURE dial to adjust the temperature to 350ºF/175ºC, and then turn the TIME dial to adjust the time to 8 minutes. 4. Press the START/STOP button to activate the function, and allow it to preheat. 5. Once preheated, insert the pan inside the oven on position 6, and then bake the food for 7 to 8 minutes. 6. When cooked, carefully remove the pan from the oven. 7. Serve and enjoy!
Per Serving: Calories 296; Fat 20.62g; Sodium 801mg; Carbs 11.54g; Fiber 4.2g; Sugar 6.32g; Protein 17.33g

Buttermilk Biscuits

Prep Time: 10 minutes | Cook Time: 5 minutes | Serves:12

2 cups all-purpose flour	butter, cut into 1-tablespoon slices
1 tablespoon baking powder	¾ cup buttermilk
¼ teaspoon baking soda	4 tablespoons (½ stick)
2 teaspoons sugar	unsalted butter, melted
1 teaspoon salt	(optional)
6 tablespoons (¾ stick) cold unsalted	

1. Spray the roasting pan with olive oil. 2. Whisk the baking soda, baking powder, sugar, flour, and salt in a mixing bowl. 3. Add butter for a coarse mixture. 4. Mix in buttermilk for a smooth mixture. 5. On a clean work surface, lightly dust with flour and roll the dough on the surface to roll into ½-inch-thick.
6. Cut the flattened dough into biscuits with a 2-inch biscuit cutter. 7. Arrange the biscuits evenly over the pan.
8. Turn the SELECT/CONFIRM dial until the indicator on the LCD screen reaches the AIRFRY function, turn the TEMPERATURE dial to adjust the temperature to 360ºF/180ºC, and then turn the TIME dial to adjust the time to 5 minutes. 9. Press the START/STOP button to activate the function, and allow it to preheat. 10. Once preheated, insert the roasting pan inside the oven on position 3 and cook the food.
11. When cooked, carefully remove from the oven and transfer to a serving platter. 12. Serve and enjoy!
Per Serving: Calories 143; Fat 6.77g; Sodium 256mg; Carbs 17.63g; Fiber 0.6g; Sugar 1.2g; Protein 3.05g

Saucy Salmon Fillets

Prep Time: 10 minutes | Cook Time: 15 minutes | Serves: 4

1 teaspoon sesame seeds	1 tablespoon minced ginger
2 tablespoons miso paste	1 teaspoon honey
2 tablespoons mirin	1 tablespoon oil, or as needed
1 tablespoon soy sauce	1-pound salmon fillets

1. Cook the sesame seeds in a saucepan over medium heat for about 2 minutes, stirring from time to time. 2. Add mirin, miso paste, ginger, and honey to a small bowl. Then add the cooked sesame seeds and stir them to combine.
3. Coat the fillets with miso, sauce. 4. Lightly grease the broiling rack with oil and line with foil, and place the coated fillets on it. 5. Insert the broiling rack inside the oven on position 2. 6. Turn the SELECT/CONFIRM dial until the indicator on the LCD screen reaches the BAKE function, turn the TEMPERATURE dial to adjust the temperature to LOW, and then turn the TIME dial to adjust the time to 15 minutes. 7. Press the START/STOP button, and broil the fillets for 10 to 15 minutes 8. When cooked, carefully remove the rack from the oven. Serve and enjoy!
Per Serving: Calories 216; Fat 10.06g; Sodium 526mg; Carbs 5.65g; Fiber 0.8g; Sugar 3.14g; Protein 24.83g

Simple Banana Bread

Prep Time: 10 minutes | Cook Time: 30 minutes | Serves: 4

1 egg
3 tablespoons brown sugar
¾ cup all-purpose flour
1 ripe banana, mashed

½ teaspoon baking soda
¼ cup sour cream
2 tablespoons butter, melted
¼ teaspoon salt

1. Select the BAKE function, and adjust the temperature at 320°F/160°C and set the time for 30 minutes. 2. Press the START/STOP button to activate the function, and allow the oven to preheat. 3. Whisk butter, egg, brown sugar, sour cream, and banana in a bowl; mix in baking soda, salt, and flour and combine well. 4. Lightly grease a loaf pan, and then pour in the batter. Place the loaf pan on the wire rack. 5. Insert the rack together with the loaf pan inside the preheated oven on position 6, and bake the loaf. 6. When the cooking time is up, carefully remove the rack from the oven. 7. Serve and enjoy!
Per Serving: Calories 292; Fat 13.39g; Sodium 447mg; Carbs 32.08g; Fiber 1.4g; Sugar 9.8g; Protein 10.94g

Banana Bread Pudding

Prep Time: 10 minutes | Cook Time: 15 minutes | Serves: 4

2 medium ripe bananas, mashed
½ cup low-fat milk
2 tablespoons maple syrup
2 tablespoons peanut butter
1 teaspoon vanilla extract

1 teaspoon ground cinnamon
2 slices whole-grain bread, cut into bite-sized cubes
¼ cup quick oats
Cooking spray

1. Lightly spritz the pizza pan over with cooking spray. 2. Mix the milk, maple syrup, peanut butter, bananas, vanilla, and cinnamon in a large bowl to incorporate. 3. Stir in the bread cubes and coat the bread cubes completely. 4. Fold in the oats and stir until well combined. Then add them into the prepared pizza pan. 5. Turn the SELECT/CONFIRM dial until the indicator on the LCD screen reaches the AIRFRY function, turn the TEMPERATURE dial to adjust the temperature to 350ºF/175ºC, and then turn the TIME dial to adjust the time to 15 minutes.6. Press the START/STOP button to activate the function, and allow it to preheat. 7. Once preheated, insert the pizza pan inside the oven on position 3. 8. Cook the food for 10 minutes and remove the pan. Then return the pan to the oven and continue cooking for 5 minutes. 9. When cooked, carefully remove it from the oven and let it cool for about 5 minutes before enjoying.
Per Serving: Calories 231; Fat 6.41g; Sodium 330mg; Carbs 35.25g; Fiber 4.1g; Sugar 16.4g; Protein 9.3g

Potato Pancakes

Prep Time: 10 minutes | Cook Time: 10 minutes | Serves: 4

1 egg
1 cup mashed potatoes
1 tablespoon garlic, minced
1 tablespoon chives, chopped
¾ cup Cheddar cheese, grated

⅓ cup flour
1 potato, grated
1 teaspoon salt

1. Select the AIRFRY function, and adjust the temperature at 400°F/200°C and set the time for 10 minutes. 2. Press the START/STOP button to activate the function, and allow the oven to preheat.3. Mix the grated potato, flour, chives, garlic, salt, egg, cheese, and mashed potatoes in a large mixing bowl. 4. Form the potato mixture into 8 equal balls. 5. Prepare a plate and line with parchment paper, and then place the potato balls on it, then slightly flatten them and place them in the freezer for 15 minutes. 6. Spray the roasting pan with cooking spray, and transfer the potato pancakes to the pan. 7. Insert the pan inside the oven on position 3. 8. Cook the potato pancakes and flip them to the other side halfway through cooking. 9. Carefully remove the pan from the oven after cooking. 10. Serve warm!
Per Serving: Calories 248; Fat 6.42g; Sodium 1084mg; Carbs 36.09g; Fiber 3.2g; Sugar 4.24g; Protein 11.79g

Zucchini-Apple Bread

Prep Time: 10 minutes | Cook Time: 30 minutes | Serves: 10

1 egg	⅓ cup walnuts, chopped
1 cup all-purpose flour	½ cup shredded zucchini
½ cup shredded apple	¾ teaspoon baking powder
1 teaspoon vanilla	1¼ teaspoons cinnamon
⅓ cup canola oil	¼ teaspoon salt
¼ teaspoon baking soda	

1. Select the BAKE function, and adjust the temperature at 325°F/165°C and set the time for 30 minutes. 2. Press the START/STOP button to activate the function, and allow the oven to preheat. 3. Mix together salt, cinnamon, baking powder, and baking soda in a bowl. 4. Whisk egg, canola oil, sugar, and vanilla in a separate bowl. 5. Mix the egg mixture and the flour mixture in the egg mixture bowl and combine well. 6. Stir in zucchini, apple, and walnuts until well combined. 7. Lightly grease an oven-proof load pan. Transfer the mixture to the pan. Place the pan on the wire rack. Then insert the rack together with the loaf pan inside the preheated oven on position 6. 8. Bake the loaf for 30 minutes. 9. When the bread has baked, carefully remove it from the oven and let it cool for about several minutes. 10. Then turn upside down the bread to a cutting board. Slice into your desired-sized slice. 11. Serve with your favored jam!
Per Serving: Calories 145; Fat 10.02g; Sodium 102mg; Carbs 11.27g; Fiber 0.8g; Sugar 0.79g; Protein 2.63g

Homemade Cheese & Sausage Burritos

Prep Time: 15 minutes | Cook Time: 25 minutes | Serves: 6

1-pound ground breakfast sausage	6 large burrito-size tortillas
8 eggs	2 cups shredded cheese of
¼ cup milk	choice
Kosher salt	6 tablespoons maple syrup
Pepper	Olive oil cooking spray
1 tablespoon butter	

1. Cook the ground sausage in the skillet over medium heat for 6 to 8 minutes, and halfway through cooking, break the sausage up. When cooked, transfer them to a plate. 2. Beat the eggs with milk, pepper, and kosher salt in a bowl for about 1 minute. 3. Melt the butter in the pan over medium-low heat, then add the egg mixture and cook for 4 to 5 minutes until the eggs are cooked and scrambled. 4. Add some cheddar, sausage, scrambled eggs, and 1 tablespoon of maple syrup to the center of each burrito, and then fold them in. Fold the top over the filling. 5. Arrange evenly 2 to 3 burritos onto the roasting pan, and spray olive oil cooking spray over both sides. 6. Turn the SELECT/CONFIRM dial until the indicator on the LCD screen reaches the AIRFRY function, turn the TEMPERATURE dial to adjust the temperature to 325°F/165°C, and then turn the TIME dial to adjust the time to 10 minutes. 7. Press the START/STOP button to activate the function, and allow it to preheat. 8. Once preheated, insert the roasting pan inside the oven on position 3, and then air fry the burritos for 10 minutes. 9. When cooked, carefully remove the pan from the oven. Serve and enjoy!
Per Serving: Calories 771; Fat 47.03g; Sodium 1260mg; Carbs 39.98g; Fiber 3.6g; Sugar 1.2g; Protein 31.27g

Crispy Chickpeas

Prep Time: 10 minutes | Cook Time: 18 minutes | Serves: 4

1 (19-ounces) can of
chickpeas, drained and
rinsed
½ teaspoon chili powder

½ teaspoon ground cumin
¼ teaspoon cayenne pepper
¼ teaspoon salt
Cooking spray

1. Select the AIRFRY function, and adjust the temperature at 390°F/200°C and set the time for 18 minutes. 2. Press the START/STOP button to activate the function, and allow the oven to preheat. 3. Line the roasting pan with parchment paper, and lightly spritz it with cooking spray. 4. Mix the chili powder, cayenne pepper, salt, and cumin in a small bowl. 5. Add chickpeas to a medium bowl and spritz them with cooking spray. 6. Mix together the spice mixture with the chickpeas and toss them to coat well. 7. Transfer the spiced chickpeas to the prepared pan, and insert the pan inside the oven on position 3. 8. Stir the chickpeas twice during baking. 9. Let the chickpeas cool for 5 minutes after baking. 10. Serve and enjoy!

Per Serving: Calories 188; Fat 3.46g; Sodium 441mg; Carbs 31.17g; Fiber 8.7g; Sugar 5.43g; Protein 9.59g

Mini Sausage Pizzas

Prep Time: 5 minutes | Cook Time: 30 minutes | Serves: 4

1-pound semolina pizza dough
3½ cups tomato sauce
1½ pounds hot Italian sausage, casings
removed and meat crumbled
8 ounces mozzarella, grated
2 tablespoons fresh thyme leaves,
chopped

½ teaspoon crushed red
pepper
¼ cup Parmigiano-
Reggiano, finely grated
Extra-virgin olive oil for
drizzling (optional)

1. Select the AIRFRY function, and adjust the temperature at 400°F/200°C and set the time for 15 minutes. 2. Press the START/STOP button to activate the function, and allow the oven to preheat. 3. Divide the dough into 4 equal parts. 4. Lightly dust flour over a work surface. Knead the 4 equal parts into an 8-inch round. 5. Add the sausage to the roasting pan. Insert the pan inside the oven in position 3, and then cook the sausage for 15 minutes. 6. When the sausage is completely cooked, carefully remove it from the pan. 7. Place dough portions on pizza pan. Spread one-quarter of the tomato sauce, mozzarella, and the cooked sausage on each dough portion. 8. Add thyme, crushed red pepper, and Parmigiano-Reggiano to garnish. 9. Allow the oven to preheat again at 400°F/200°C on PIZZA cooking mode.10. Insert the pan inside the oven on position 7, and cook them for 15 minutes or more until crispy (you can cook them in batches). 11. Drizzle with some extra olive oil to serve as you like.

Per Serving: Calories 859; Fat 24.19g; Sodium 2558mg; Carbs 108.3g; Fiber 12g; Sugar 8.49g; Protein 57.79g

Stuffed Red Potatoes

Prep Time: 10 minutes | Cook Time: 20 minutes | Serves: 6

12 small red potatoes
1 teaspoon kosher salt, divided
1 tablespoon extra-virgin olive oil

¼ cup grated sharp Cheddar cheese
¼ cup sour cream
2 tablespoons chopped chives
2 tablespoons grated Parmesan cheese

1. Select the ROAST function, and adjust the temperature at 375°F/190°C and set the time for 15 minutes. 2. Press the START/STOP button to activate the function, and allow the oven to preheat. 3. Coat the potatoes with ½ teaspoon of salt and olive oil in a bowl. 4. Evenly arrange the potatoes in the roasting pan, insert the pan inside the preheated oven on position 6, and then roast them for 15 minutes. 5. After 10 minutes of cooking time, flip the potatoes and continue cooking. 6. When done, remove the pan from the oven and let the potatoes rest for 5 minutes. 7. Halve the potatoes lengthwise. 8. Using a spoon, scoop the potato into a bowl, leaving a thin shell of skin. Arrange the potato halves on the Baking Pan. 9. Mash the potato flesh until smooth. Stir in the remaining ½ teaspoon of the salt, Cheddar cheese, sour cream, and chives. 10. Spoon the filling into the potato shells. 11. Sprinkle with Parmesan cheese. 12. Roast them at the same temperature for 5 minutes. 13. When cooking is complete, the tops should be browning slightly. 14. Remove the potatoes and let them cool slightly before serving.
Per Serving: Calories 585; Fat 6.72g; Sodium 639mg; Carbs 118.5g; Fiber 12.6g; Sugar 9.59g; Protein 17.09g

Spinach Rolls

Prep Time: 15 minutes | Cook Time: 25 minutes | Serves: 4-6

7 ounces of baby spinach
1 clove of minced garlic
10 ounces Ricotta
⅓ cup Parmesan
1 cup shredded cheddar cheese

2 eggs
2 green onions
Salt & pepper to taste
Thawed frozen puff pastry, 2 sheets

1. Select the AIRFRY function, and adjust the temperature at 390°F/200°C and set the time for 20 minutes. 2. Press the START/STOP button to activate the function, and allow the oven to preheat. 3. Add oil in a skillet and heat it over medium heat. 4. Add garlic and cook for 30 seconds, stirring from time to time. 5. Add spinach in the skillet and cook for 3 minutes or more. Add salt. Set aside for later use. 6. Add Cheddar cheese, Parmesan cheese, 1 egg, green onion, and ricotta in a mixing bowl and mix in spinach. Combine well. 7. Half the puff pastry and fill the puff pastry halves with the spinach mixture. 8. Brush beaten egg liquid over sides and roll tightly into logs. 10. Place the rolls in the refrigerator for 15 minutes. 11. Then cut them into 4 pieces and brush with beaten egg liquid. Place the pieces in the air fryer basket and insert the basket inside the preheated oven on position 3. 12. Cook the rolls for 15 to 20 minutes. 13. When the cooking time is up, carefully remove it from the oven. 14. Serve and enjoy!
Per Serving: Calories 298; Fat 17.26g; Sodium 595mg; Carbs 19.92g; Fiber 1.7g; Sugar 5.11g; Protein 16.67g

Easy Plantain Pieces

Prep Time: 10 minutes | Cook Time: 10 minutes | Serves: 2

2 ripe plantains, peeled and cut at a diagonal into ½-inch-thick pieces

3 tablespoons ghee, melted
¼ teaspoon kosher salt

1. Select the AIRFRY function, and adjust the temperature at 400°F/200°C and set the time for 8 minutes. 2. Press the START/STOP button to activate the function, and allow the oven to preheat. 3. Coat the plantains with salt and ghee in a bowl. 4. Transfer the seasoned plantains to the air fryer basket, arranging them as evenly as possible. 5. Insert the basket inside the preheated oven on position 3. 6. When done, the plantains should be soft on the inside and crispy on the outside. 7. Carefully remove them from the oven, and serve and enjoy.

Per Serving: Calories 371; Fat 17.94g; Sodium 435mg; Carbs 57.1g; Fiber 4.1g; Sugar 26.86g; Protein 2.51g

Jicama Strips

Prep Time: 10 minutes | Cook Time: 5 minutes | Serves: 4

1 tablespoon dried thyme
¾ cup arrowroot flour

½ large jicama, sliced
2 eggs

1. Select the AIRFRY function, and adjust the temperature at 350°F/175°C and set the time for 5 minutes. 2. Press the START/STOP button to activate the function, and allow the oven to preheat.3. Pour the whisked eggs over the jicama and toss them to coat well; add thyme, arrowroot, and a pinch of salt and mix well. 4. Toss the coated jicama together with the thyme mixture until well coated. 5. Spray the air fryer basket with olive oil, place the jicama fries in it, and insert it inside the preheated oven on position 3. 6. Toss the fries several times during cooking to cook evenly. 7. Carefully remove them from the oven. Serve and enjoy!

Per Serving: Calories 175; Fat 2.26g; Sodium 38mg; Carbs 34.69g; Fiber 8.3g; Sugar 2.78g; Protein 3.95g

Baked Pumpkin Seeds

Prep Time: 10 minutes | Cook Time: 40 minutes | Serves: 4

1 cup pumpkin seeds, pulp removed, rinsed
1 tablespoon butter, melted
1 tablespoon brown sugar

1 teaspoon orange zest
½ teaspoon cardamom
½ teaspoon salt

1. Select the BAKE function, and adjust the temperature at 320°F/160°C and set the time for 4 minutes. 2. Press the START/STOP button to activate the function, and allow the oven to preheat. 3. Once preheated, add the pumpkin seeds to the roasting pan and insert the pan inside the air fryer on position 6; bake the pumpkin seeds for 4 minutes. 4. While baking the pumpkin seeds, mix the sugar, orange zest, salt, cardamom, and melted butter in a bowl. 5. Toss together the seeds and the cardamom mixture in the bowl to coat well, and then transfer them to the roasting pan. 6. Return the seeds to the oven, and then bake them at 300°F/150°C for 35 minutes, tossing them every 10 to 12 minutes. 7. Carefully remove from the oven. Serve and enjoy!

Per Serving: Calories 204; Fat 17.37g; Sodium 389mg; Carbs 6.66g; Fiber 2g; Sugar 2.45g; Protein 8.87g

Simple French Fries

Prep Time: 10 minutes | Cook Time: 16 minutes | Serves: 2

½ pound potatoes, peeled and cut into ½-inch thick sticks lengthwise
1 tablespoon olive oil
Salt and ground black pepper to taste

1. Select the AIRFRY function, and adjust the temperature at 400°F/200°C and set the time for 16 minutes. 2. Press the START/STOP button to activate the function, and allow the oven to preheat. 3. Mix all of the ingredients in a large mixing bowl to coat the potatoes well. 4. Transfer the coated potato sticks to the air fryer basket and then air fry them on position 3 for 16 minutes. 5. When done, carefully remove the basket from the oven. Serve and enjoy!
Per Serving: Calories 150; Fat 6.89g; Sodium 7mg; Carbs 20.55g; Fiber 2.8g; Sugar 0.89g; Protein 2.41g

Tasty Cauliflower Fritters

Prep Time: 10 minutes | Cook Time: 14 minutes | Serves: 8

½ cup chopped parsley	cheddar cheese
1 cup Italian breadcrumbs	1 egg
⅓ cup shredded mozzarella cheese	2 minced garlic cloves
⅓ cup shredded sharp	3 chopped scallions
	1 head of cauliflower, cut into florets

1. Select the BAKE function, and adjust the temperature at 390°F/200°C and set the time for 14 minutes. 2. Press the START/STOP button to activate the function, and allow the oven to preheat. 3. Wash the cauliflower florets and pat them dry. 4. Pulse the cauliflower florets in a food processor for 20 to 30 seconds to 'rice.' 5. Add the cauliflower rice into a bowl, and then add salt, cheeses, breadcrumbs, garlic, scallions, and eggs. Mix them well. 6. Form 15 patties from the mixture, adding more breadcrumbs as needed. Finally, spritz the patties with olive oil and arrange them evenly on the roasting pan in a single layer. 7. Cook the patties in the preheated oven and flip them once halfway through cooking. 8. Serve and enjoy!
Per Serving: Calories 83; Fat 4.35g; Sodium 227mg; Carbs 4.87g; Fiber 1.2g; Sugar 1.37g; Protein 6.58g

Sweet Potato Chips

Prep Time: 10 minutes | Cook Time: 8 minutes | Serves: 2

1 small sweet potato, cut into ⅜-inch-thick slices	2 teaspoons ground cinnamon
2 tablespoons olive oil	

1. Select the AIRFRY function, and adjust the temperature at 390°F/200°C and set the time for 8 minutes. 2. Press the START/STOP button to activate the function, and allow the oven to preheat. 3. Toss the potato slices and olive oil together in a bowl until the slices are well coated; stir in cinnamon and combine well. 4. Add the sweet potato to the air fryer basket and insert the oven inside the air fryer on position 3. Cook them and stir halfway through cooking. 5. Let them cool for about 5 minutes after cooking. 6. Serve and enjoy!
Per Serving: Calories 153; Fat 13.58g; Sodium 11mg; Carbs 8.31g; Fiber 2.4g; Sugar 2g; Protein 0.71g

Air Fried Potato Pieces

Prep Time: 10 minutes | Cook Time: 20 minutes | Serves: 4

3-4 russet potatoes peel and chop into
1-inch pieces
2-3 tablespoons olive oil
1 teaspoon salt

1 teaspoon garlic powder
½ teaspoon onion powder
½ teaspoon sweet paprika
Cooking spray

1. Select the AIRFRY function, and adjust the temperature at 400°F/200°C and set the time for 20 minutes. 2. Press the START/STOP button to activate the function, and allow the oven to preheat. 3. Coat the potatoes with the garlic powder, onion powder, sweet paprika, salt, and olive oil in a large bowl. 4. Spritz the roasting pan with non-stick cooking spray, and then arrange the potato pieces to the pan in single layer. 5. Once preheated, insert the pan inside the oven on position 3. 6. Cook the potato pieces, and shake them once or more halfway through cooking. 7. When the potatoes have cooked, carefully remove them from the oven. 8. Serve and enjoy!

Per Serving: Calories 334; Fat 8.76g; Sodium 599mg; Carbs 59.31g; Fiber 4.4g; Sugar 2.07g; Protein 7.11g

Tasty Cheese Sticks

Prep Time: 10 minutes | Cook Time: 70 minutes | Serves: 4

(6) 1 ounce of mozzarella
string cheese sticks, cut in
half
½ ounces of pork rinds,

finely ground
2 large eggs
½ cup grated Parmesan cheese
1 teaspoon dried parsley

1. Select the AIRFRY function, and adjust the temperature at 400°F/200°C and set the time for 10 minutes. 2. Press the START/STOP button to activate the function, and allow the oven to preheat. 3. Place the sticks in a freezer and freeze them overnight until they are firm. 4. Add ground pork rinds, parsley, and parmesan to a large bowl and mix well. 5. Whisk eggs in a bowl. 6. Dip the frozen mozzarella sticks first in the whisked eggs, and then coat well with the parmesan mixture. Repeat with the remaining sticks. 7. Transfer the mozzarella sticks onto the roasting pan and insert the pan inside the oven on position 3. 8. Cook them until golden. 9. Serve and enjoy!

Per Serving: Calories 99; Fat 6.37g; Sodium 285mg; Carbs 2.31g; Fiber 0.1g; Sugar 0.16g; Protein 8.05g

Homemade Potato Chips

Prep Time: 15 minutes | Cook Time: 25 minutes | Serves: 4

4 medium yellow potatoes cut into thin
slices

1 tablespoon oil
Salt to taste

1. Select the AIRFRY function, and adjust the temperature at 200°F/95°C and set the time for 20 minutes. 2. Press the START/STOP button to activate the function, and allow the oven to preheat. 3. Soak the potato slices in a bowl with cold water for at least 20 minutes. 4. Drain and pat them dry. 5. Toss the potato slice with salt and olive oil, and then place them in the air fryer basket. 6. Insert the basket inside the preheated oven on position 3, and cook the potato slices for 20 minutes.7. When the cooking has done, toss the potato chips and continue cooking for 5 minutes at 400°F/200°C. 8. Carefully remove the basket from the oven. 9. Serve and enjoy!

Per Serving: Calories 194; Fat 3.59g; Sodium 52mg; Carbs 37.21g; Fiber 4.7g; Sugar 1.66g; Protein 4.3g

Ravioli

Prep Time: 5 minutes | Cook Time: 10 minutes | Serves: 1

12 frozen ravioli   ½ cup Italian breadcrumbs
½ cup Buttermilk

1. Select the AIRFRY function, and adjust the temperature at 400°F/200°C and set the time for 7 minutes. 2. Press the START/STOP button to activate the function, and allow the oven to preheat. 3. Add buttermilk in a bowl. Then, in a separate bowl, add breadcrumbs. 4. Dip the ravioli first in the buttermilk and then in the breadcrumbs. 5. Arrange the ravioli evenly in the air fryer basket and then insert them inside the preheated oven on position 3. 6. Cook them for 7 minutes and spray them with oil halfway. 7. Carefully remove from the oven. 8. Serve and enjoy!
Per Serving: Calories 370; Fat 12.76g; Sodium 377mg; Carbs 32.47g; Fiber 0.3g; Sugar 7.26g; Protein 31.97g

Baked Crackers

Prep Time: 25 minutes | Cook Time: 11 minutes | Serves: 4-5

2-½ cups all-purpose flour   1 to 2 tablespoons minced
½ cup white whole wheat flour   fresh thyme
1 teaspoon salt   ¾ teaspoon sea or kosher
¾ cup water   salt
¼ cup plus 1 tablespoon olive oil

1. Select the BAKE function, and adjust the temperature at 375°F/190°C and set the time for 11 minutes. 2. Press the START/STOP button to activate the function, and allow the oven to preheat. 3. Add flour and salt to a large bowl and whisk well. 4. Gradually add water and ¼ cup oil and toss until firm dough has formed. 5. Divide the dough into three portions. 6. Knead the dough into a ⅛-inch thick and cut with a 1 to ½-in round cookie cutter. 7. Place them in the roasting pan inside and insert inside the oven on position 6. 8. Prick each cracker with a fork and brush lightly with the rest oil. 9. Sprinkle thyme and sea salt over the crackers. 10. Bake them in the oven for 9 to 11 minutes. 11. Serve and enjoy after baking!
Per Serving: Calories 202; Fat 5.08g; Sodium 908mg; Carbs 33.51g; Fiber 1.2g; Sugar 0.12g; Protein 4.59g

Bacon Wrapped Avocado

Prep Time: 10 minutes | Cook Time: 20 minutes | Serves: 4-6

2 medium ripe avocados   2 to 3 tablespoons Sriracha chili sauce
12 bacon strips   1 to 2 tablespoons Lime juice
Sauce   1 teaspoon grated lime zest
½ cup Mayonnaise

1. Select the BAKE function, and adjust the temperature at 400°F/200°C and set the time for 15 minutes. 2. Press the START/STOP button to activate the function, and allow the oven to preheat. 3. Peel the avocado and remove their pits. Cut them into half, and then cut each half into three wedges. 4. Wrap each wedge with a bacon strip. 5. Place the wrapped wedges evenly in the roasting pan in a single layer. 6. Insert the pan inside the preheated oven on position 6. 7. While the wedges are cooking, make the sauce mixing mayonnaise, lime juice, and lime zest. 8. Carefully remove from the oven and transfer to a serving plate. 9. Serve the mayo-lime sauce. Enjoy!
Per Serving: Calories 209; Fat 19.15g; Sodium 382mg; Carbs 8.37g; Fiber 5.3g; Sugar 1.27g; Protein 3.75g

Breaded Zucchini Sticks

Prep Time: 30 minutes | Cook Time: 15 minutes | Serves: 4

3 medium zucchini, cut into strips
Salt
½ cup gluten-free breadcrumbs
¼ cup nutritional yeast
1 tablespoon granulated garlic

1 tablespoon dried parsley
½ teaspoon salt
1 egg, beaten
Cooking spray
3 tablespoons olive oil

1. Select the AIRFRY function, and adjust the temperature at 400°F/200°C and set the time for 15 minutes. 2. Press the START/STOP button to activate the function, and allow the oven to preheat. 3. Place the zucchini strips in a pan and add salt. Allow it to sit for about 20 minutes. Then pat them dry. 4. Add nutritional yeast, breadcrumbs, salt, and parsley to a mixing bowl and mix well. 5. Beat the eggs in a shallow bowl. 6. Dip the zucchini stick first in the beaten eggs and then coat thoroughly with the breadcrumbs. 7. Place the coated zucchini sticks in the air fryer basket. Brush the top with oil and then insert the basket inside the preheat oven on position 3. 8. Cook them and turn over to brush the other side halfway through. 9. Carefully remove the basket from the oven after cooking. 10. Serve and enjoy!

Per Serving: Calories 158; Fat 11.47g; Sodium 903mg; Carbs 7.86g; Fiber 1.4g; Sugar 0.5g; Protein 6.36g

Chicken Tenders

Prep Time: 10 minutes | Cook Time: 10 minutes | Serves: 4

12 ounces chicken breasts
1 egg white
⅛ cup flour

1¼ ounces Panko breadcrumbs
Salt and pepper

1. Select the AIRFRY function, and adjust the temperature at 350°F/175°C and set the time for 10 minutes. 2. Press the START/STOP button to activate the function, and allow the oven to preheat. 3. Remove the fat parts from the chicken breast and chip them into tenders. 4. Toss the chicken tender with salt and pepper to season evenly. 5. Dip the chicken tenders first in flour, then in the egg whites, and finally coat them with the Panko breadcrumbs. 6. Spray the air fryer basket with olive oil and evenly arrange the chicken tenders in it. Then, insert the basket inside the preheated oven on position 3. 7. Air fry the chicken tenders in the oven until thoroughly cooked. 8. Carefully remove the basket from the oven. 9. Serve and enjoy!

Per Serving: Calories 205; Fat 8.43g; Sodium 176mg; Carbs 10.66g; Fiber 0.7g; Sugar 1.42g; Protein 20.4g

Breaded Avocado Fries

Prep Time: 10 minutes | Cook Time: 20 minutes | Serves: 4

½ cup Panko breadcrumbs
½ teaspoon salt
1 Hass avocado - peeled, pitted, and sliced

Aquafaba from a 15-ounce can of white beans or garbanzo beans

1. Select the AIRFRY function, and adjust the temperature at 390°F/200°C and set the time for 10 minutes. 2. Press the START/STOP button to activate the function, and allow the oven to preheat. 3. Add salt and breadcrumbs in a small bowl and toss them together. 4. Half fill a separate bowl with aquafaba and dredge in avocado slices. 5. Then add the avocado fries to the Panko breadcrumbs and press to coat evenly. 6. Arrange the avocado fries onto the air fryer basket. Insert the basket inside the preheated oven on position 3. 7. Air fry them in your oven for 10 minutes and shake once halfway through cooking. 8. When the cooking time is up, carefully remove the basket from the oven. 9. Serve and enjoy!

Per Serving: Calories 184; Fat 11.48g; Sodium 395mg; Carbs 16.98g; Fiber 4.1g; Sugar 1.17g; Protein 4.72g

Roasted Chickpeas

Prep Time: 5 minutes | Cook Time: 20 minutes | Serves: 8

1 (15-ounce) can of chickpeas - drained but not rinsed and save the liquid from the can	4 teaspoons dried dill
	2 teaspoons garlic powder
	2 teaspoons onion powder
	¾ teaspoon sea salt
1 tablespoon olive oil	1 tablespoon lemon juice

1. Select the ROAST function, and adjust the temperature at 400°F/200°C and set the time for 12 minutes. 2. Press the START/STOP button to activate the function, and allow the oven to preheat. 3. Add 1 tablespoon of the reserved liquid from the chickpea can in a mixing bowl and the chickpeas and toss well. 4. Add the chickpeas as well as the liquid to the roasting pan. Then, insert the pan into the preheated oven on position 6. 5. Let it roast. When the cooking has done, transfer the chickpeas back to the small bowl and add olive oil, garlic powder, dill, salt, lemon juice, and onion powder. Toss to coat the beans evenly. 6. Adjust the temperature to 350°F/175°C and time to 5 minutes. 7. Roast the chickpeas in your oven. 8. When the cooking time is up, carefully remove it from the oven. 9. Serve and enjoy! Or reserve cooled in an airtight container.
Per Serving: Calories 50; Fat 3.66g; Sodium 220mg; Carbs 3.32g; Fiber 0.4g; Sugar 0.11g; Protein 1.38g

Exotic Chicken Meatballs

Prep Time: 10 minutes | Cook Time: 10 minutes | Serves: 4

½ cup sweet chili sauce	1 tablespoon minced fresh cilantro
2 tablespoons lime juice	
2 tablespoons ketchup	½ teaspoon salt
1 teaspoon soy sauce	½ teaspoon garlic powder
1 large egg, lightly beaten	1 pound lean ground chicken
¾ cup Panko bread crumbs	
1 finely chopped green onion	

1. Select the AIRFRY function, and adjust the temperature at 350°F/175°C and set the time for 10 minutes. 2. Press the START/STOP button to activate the function, and allow the oven to preheat. 3. Add chili sauce, soy sauce, ketchup, and lime juice to a small bowl. 4. Mix egg, cilantro, green onion, garlic powder, the remaining chili sauce, and breadcrumbs in a large bowl. 5. Then add chicken and combine well. Make the mixture into 12 balls. 6. Evenly arrange the meatballs into the air fryer basket in a single layer, and insert the basket inside the preheated oven on position 3. 7. Cook the meatballs and turn them halfway through cooking. 8. Carefully remove the basket from the oven after cooking. 9. Serve and enjoy!
Per Serving: Calories 249; Fat 10.98g; Sodium 950mg; Carbs 14.82g; Fiber 2.6g; Sugar 6.89g; Protein 22.34g

Mac & Cheese Balls

Prep Time: 15 minutes | Cook Time: 20 minutes | Serves: 4

1 cup Panko breadcrumbs	1 teaspoon smoked paprika, divided
4 cups prepared macaroni and cheese, refrigerated	½ teaspoon garlic powder, divided
	2 eggs
3 tablespoons flour	1 tablespoon milk
1 teaspoon salt, divided	¼ cup ranch dressing, garlic aioli, or chipotle mayo for dipping, optional
1 teaspoon ground black pepper, divided	

1. Select the BAKE function, and adjust the temperature at 370°F/190°C and set the time for 5 minutes. 2. Press the START/STOP button to activate the function, and allow the oven to preheat. 3. On the roasting pan, add the breadcrumbs and shake them to an even layer. 4. Insert the pan inside the preheated oven on position 6. 5. Bake the breadcrumbs in the oven for 3 minutes. Shake and bake them for 1 or 2 minutes until the crumbs are completely toasted. 6. Make the prepared macaroni and cheese into medium-sized balls. Then arrange them onto the pan. 7. Add ½ teaspoon of salt, ½ teaspoon of black pepper, ½ teaspoon of smoked paprika, ¼ teaspoon of garlic powder, and flour in a suitable bowl and whisk together.
8. In a shallow bowl, add 2 eggs and milk and whisk well. 9. Toss the bread crumbs with salt, paprika, garlic powder, and pepper.
10. Dip the mac and cheese balls in the flour mixture and coat well. Then drop in the egg mixture, rolling to coat. Coat them with the breadcrumbs, patting to coat well.11. Spritz the air fryer basket with cooking spray. Arrange the mar and cheese balls evenly in the air fryer basket and spritz the balls with cooking spray. Next, insert it inside the preheated oven on position 3. 12. Air fry the balls in the oven at 370°F/190°C for 8 to 10 minutes. 13. Air fry until the balls are golden brown and crispy. Repeat with the remaining balls.
14. Carefully remove the basket from the oven. 15. Serve and enjoy!
Per Serving: Calories 652; Fat 14.8g; Sodium 974mg; Carbs 104.91g; Fiber 5.2g; Sugar 5.79g; Protein 22.92g

Chapter 3 Vegetables and Sides Recipes

Cheese Tomato Halves

Prep Time: 10 minutes | Cook Time: 15 minutes | Serves: 4

4 large tomatoes, halved
¼ cup fresh oregano, chopped
¼ cup fresh basil, chopped

½ cup mozzarella cheese, shredded
¼ cup Parmesan cheese, grated
Pepper
Salt

1. Select the BAKE function, and adjust the temperature at 450°F/230°C and set the time for 15 minutes. 2. Press the START/STOP button to activate the function, and allow the oven to preheat. 3. Arrange the tomato halves to the roasting pan, cut-side up. Top the tomato halves with parmesan cheese, mozzarella cheese, basil, oregano, salt, and pepper. 4. Insert the pan inside the preheated oven on position 6, and then bake the food for 15 minutes. 5. When done, transfer the food to the serving plate.
Per Serving: Calories 82; Fat 2.15g; Sodium 266mg; Carbs 9.16g; Fiber 2.8g; Sugar 5.03g; Protein 8g

Carrots & Turnips

Prep Time: 10 minutes | Cook Time: 25 minutes | Serves: 4

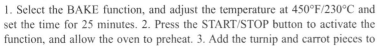

1-pound turnips, peeled and cut into 1–2-inch pieces
1-pound carrots, peeled and cut into 1–2-inch pieces
2 tablespoons canola oil

1 tablespoon dried herbs
2 garlic cloves, sliced
Pepper
Salt

1. Select the BAKE function, and adjust the temperature at 450°F/230°C and set the time for 25 minutes. 2. Press the START/STOP button to activate the function, and allow the oven to preheat. 3. Add the turnip and carrot pieces to a large and deep bowl, and then toss them with the oil, dried herbs, garlic, salt, and pepper. 4. Spread them onto the roasting pan, and then insert the pan inside the preheated oven on position 6. 5. Bake them in the oven and stir them halfway through. 6. When done, transfer the food to the serving plate.
Per Serving: Calories 152; Fat 7.73g; Sodium 139mg; Carbs 17.23g; Fiber 6.9g; Sugar 6.61g; Protein 4.6g

Cheese Broccoli Casserole

Prep Time: 10 minutes | Cook Time: 10 minutes | Serves: 6

20 ounces fresh broccoli florets, steamed
¼ cup Monterey jack cheese, shredded
1 tablespoon ranch seasoning

¼ cup sour cream
1 cup cheddar cheese, shredded
8 ounces cream cheese, softened
Pepper
Salt

1. Select the BAKE function, and adjust the temperature at 350°F/175°C and set the time for 10 minutes. 2. Press the START/STOP button to activate the function, and allow the oven to preheat. 3. Combine the broccoli, ranch seasoning, sour cream, cheddar cheese, cream cheese, salt, and pepper in a bowl. 4. Transfer the mixture to the roasting pan, and then top with the shredded Monterey jack cheese. 5. Insert the pan inside the oven on position 6, and bake them for 10 minutes. 6. When done, transfer the food to the serving plate.
Per Serving: Calories 238; Fat 17.32g; Sodium 783mg; Carbs 9.86g; Fiber 2.8g; Sugar 4.56g; Protein 12.53g

Acorn Squash Slices

Prep Time: 10 minutes | Cook Time: 15 minutes | Serves: 4

1 acorn squash, seeds removed and cut into slices
1 stick butter, melted

¼ cup maple syrup
¼ teaspoon kosher salt

1. Select the AIRFRY function, and adjust the temperature at 400°F/200°C and set the time for 15 minutes. 2. Press the START/STOP button to activate the function, and allow the oven to preheat. 3. Toss the acorn squash slices with maple syrup, salt, and butter, then arrange the acorn squash slices in the air fryer basket. 4. Insert the basket inside the oven on position 3, and cook them for 15 minutes. 5. Turn the slices halfway through. 6. When the time is up, allow the food to cool slightly before serving.
Per Serving: Calories 297; Fat 23.03g; Sodium 333mg; Carbs 24.45g; Fiber 1.6g; Sugar 11.93g; Protein 1.11g

Brussels Sprouts

Prep Time: 10 minutes | Cook Time: 20 minutes | Serves: 4

1-pound Brussels sprouts cut in half
1 teaspoon canola oil
1 tablespoon garlic, minced
3 teaspoons lime juice for serving

2 tablespoons sweet chili sauce for serving
Pepper
Salt

1. Select the AIRFRY function, and adjust the temperature at 400°F/200°C and set the time for 20 minutes. 2. Press the START/STOP button to activate the function, and allow the oven to preheat. 3. Add the Brussels sprouts to the air fryer basket and then toss them with the oil, garlic, salt, and pepper. 4. Insert the basket inside the oven on position 3, and cook the Brussels sprouts for 20 minutes. 5. Stir the Brussels sprouts halfway through. 6. When cooked, transfer the Brussels sprouts to the bowl, add the sweet chili sauce and lime juice to the bowl and toss them well.
Per Serving: Calories 77; Fat 1.5g; Sodium 100mg; Carbs 14.88g; Fiber 4.5g; Sugar 4.22g; Protein 4.07g

Fried Tofu Cubes

Prep Time: 5 minutes | Cook Time: 25 minutes | Serves: 4

16 ounces firm tofu, pressed and cubed
1 tablespoon vegan oyster sauce
1 tablespoon tamari sauce
1 teaspoon cider vinegar
1 teaspoon pure maple

syrup
1 teaspoon sriracha
½ teaspoon shallot powder
½ teaspoon porcini powder
1 teaspoon garlic powder
1 tablespoon sesame oil
2 tablespoons golden flaxseed meal

1. Select the BAKE function, and adjust the temperature at 365°F/185°C and set the time for 22 minutes. 2. Press the START/STOP button to activate the function, and allow the oven to preheat. 3. Mix the tofu with the remaining ingredients in a bowl and then allow the tofu to marinate for 30 minutes. 4. Place the coated tofu in the roasting pan, and insert the pan inside the preheated oven on position 6, then bake them for 22 minutes. 5. After 10 minutes of cooking time, flip the food and cook for 12 minutes longer.6. Serve warm.
Per Serving: Calories 233; Fat 15.49g; Sodium 182mg; Carbs 8.94g; Fiber 4.2g; Sugar 1.35g; Protein 19.12g

Herbed Head Cauliflower

Prep Time: 10 minutes | Cook Time: 10 minutes | Serves: 4

1 medium head cauliflower, cut into florets (about 6 cups)	1 teaspoon grated lemon zest
4 tablespoons olive oil, divided	2 tablespoons lemon juice
¼ cup minced fresh parsley	½ teaspoon salt
1 tablespoon minced fresh rosemary	¼ teaspoon crushed red pepper flakes
1 tablespoon chopped fresh thyme	

1. Select the AIRFRY function, and adjust the temperature at 350°F/175°C and set the time for 10 minutes. 2. Press the START/STOP button to activate the function, and allow the oven to preheat. 3. Add the cauliflower florets to a large bowl and then evenly coat them with 2 tablespoons of olive oil. 4. Arrange the cauliflower florets in batches in a single layer on the roasting pan. 5. Insert the pan inside the oven on position 3, and cook them for 10 minutes. 6. Stir halfway through and cook until the florets are tender and the edges are browned. 7. While cooking the cauliflower florets, mix up the remaining ingredients in a bowl. 8. Transfer the cooked cauliflower florets to the serving plate, drizzle them with the mixture and toss them to combine.
Per Serving: Calories 142; Fat 13.78g; Sodium 313mg; Carbs 4.65g; Fiber 1.7g; Sugar 1.67g; Protein 1.52g

Green Beans and Mushrooms

Prep Time: 15 minutes | Cook Time: 20 minutes | Serves: 6

1 pound fresh green beans cut into 2 inch pieces	and thinly sliced
½ pound sliced fresh mushrooms	2 tablespoons olive oil
	1 teaspoon Italian seasoning
1 small red onion, halved	¼ teaspoon salt
	⅛ teaspoon pepper

1. Select the AIRFRY function, and adjust the temperature at 375°F/190°C and set the time for 20 minutes. 2. Press the START/STOP button to activate the function, and allow the oven to preheat. 3. Add all the ingredients to a large bowl and then toss them to coat the green beans well. 4. Grease the roasting pan with oil or cooking spray. 5. Arrange the food in the pan, and cook them for 20 minutes, tossing halfway through cooking. 6. Serve warm.
Per Serving: Calories 82; Fat 4.79g; Sodium 154mg; Carbs 8.17g; Fiber 3g; Sugar 3.12g; Protein 2.38g

Spicy Okra Fries

Prep Time: 10 minutes | Cook Time: 15 minutes | Serves: 4

15 ounces okra, wash & pat dry	2 tablespoons canola oil
½ teaspoon garlic powder	1 teaspoon paprika
1 teaspoon chili powder	Pepper
Salt	

1. Select the AIRFRY function, and adjust the temperature at 400°F/200°C and set the time for 15 minutes. 2. Press the START/STOP button to activate the function, and allow the oven to preheat. 3. Mix up all the ingredients in the bowl to coat the okra well. 4. Place the coated okra in the air fryer basket, insert the basket inside the oven on position 3, and then cook them for 15 minutes. 5. Toss the okra halfway through cooking. 6. Serve warm.
Per Serving: Calories 103; Fat 7.39g; Sodium 66mg; Carbs 9.23g; Fiber 4g; Sugar 1.69g; Protein 2.35g

Tasty Falafels with Tahini Sauce

Prep Time: 10 minutes | Cook Time: 35 minutes | Serves: 20

½ medium yellow onion, cut into quarters
4 cloves garlic
¼ cup packed parsley leaves
¼ cup packed cilantro leaves
2 (15 ounces) cans chickpeas, rinsed and

drained
1 teaspoon kosher salt
1 teaspoon baking powder
1 teaspoon dried coriander
½ teaspoon crushed red pepper flakes

For Tahini Sauce
⅓ cup tahini
Juice of ½ a lemon
3 tablespoon water, plus more as needed

Pinch of kosher salt
Pinch of red pepper flakes

1. Select the AIRFRY function, and adjust the temperature at 370°F/185°C and set the time for 15 minutes. 2. Press the START/STOP button to activate the function, and allow the oven to preheat. 3. Put the onion, garlic, parsley, and cilantro into the food processor and then pulse them until coarsely chopped, scraping down edges as required. 4. Add the chickpeas, baking powder, coriander, cumin, red pepper flakes, and salt, and pulse until the chickpeas are mostly broken done but still have a few pieces. 5. Stop the processor just as the mixture starts to turn into a paste. 6. Scoop out about two tablespoons of the mixture and gently roll it into a ball. Do the same with the remaining mixture. 7. Arrange the falafels in the air fryer basket, and insert the basket inside the oven on position 3. 8. Cook the falafels for 15 minutes. 9. While cooking the falafels, combine the tahini and lemon juice in the bowl; stir in the water until the tahini mixture is completely mixed, one tablespoon at a time. 10. Add the salt and red pepper flakes to the tahini mixture. 11. Serve the falafels with tahini sauce.
Per Serving: Calories 57; Fat 2.74g; Sodium 182mg; Carbs 6.66g; Fiber 1.9g; Sugar 1.21g; Protein 2.34g

Onion Cauliflower Tacos

Prep Time: 25 minutes | Cook Time: 70 minutes | Serves: 4

For The Slaw
1 cup thinly sliced red cabbage
½ small red onion, diced
1 jalapeño, minced
For The Cauliflower
1-½ cups all-purpose flour
1 teaspoon chili powder
1 teaspoon cumin
½ teaspoon garlic powder
½ teaspoon cayenne pepper
Kosher salt
Freshly ground black
For Serving
½ cup vegan mayonnaise
2 tablespoons Sriracha
1 teaspoon maple syrup
Corn tortillas

1 clove of garlic, minced
Juice of 1 lime
2 tablespoons apple cider vinegar
Pinch of kosher salt

pepper
1-½ cups almond milk or other non-dairy milk
1-½ cups Panko breadcrumbs
1 medium head cauliflower, cut into bite-size florets
Cooking spray

Sliced avocado
Freshly chopped cilantro
Lime wedges

1. Select the AIRFRY function, and adjust the temperature at 400°F/200°C and set the time for 15 minutes. 2. Press the START/STOP button to activate the function, and allow the oven to preheat. 3. Mix up all the slaw ingredients in a bowl, and then allow the mixture to sit while preparing tacos, stirring occasionally. 4. Combine the flour, cumin, chili powder, garlic powder, cayenne pepper, salt, and pepper in the second bowl, and stir in the almond milk until the mixture is thick but not too thick. 5. Add the Panko to the third bowl. 6. Dip the florets into the milk mixture, wiping off any excess, then into the Panko. 7. Spray the covered cauliflower with cooking spray and place them in the roasting pan, insert the pan inside the oven on position 3. 8. Cook the cauliflower for 15 minutes. 9. Toss the cauliflower halfway through and spray with extra cooking spray. 10. Mix up the vegan mayonnaise, sriracha, and maple syrup in a small bowl. 11. Place the cauliflower, avocado, pickled slaw, cilantro, and a drizzle of sriracha mayo on the top of the tortilla. Serve with lime wedges.
Per Serving: Calories 410; Fat 17.49g; Sodium 608mg; Carbs 55.45g; Fiber 7.8g; Sugar 10.73g; Protein 10.79g

Parmesan Eggplant

Prep Time: 20 minutes | Cook Time: 10 minutes | Serves: 4

1 large eggplant mine was around 1.25 pounds
½ cup whole wheat bread crumbs
3 tablespoons finely grated Parmesan cheese
Salt to taste
1 teaspoon Italian seasoning mix
3 tablespoons whole wheat flour

1 egg + 1 tablespoon of water
Olive oil spray
1 cup marinara sauce
¼ cup grated Mozzarella cheese
Fresh parsley or basil to garnish

1. Select the AIRFRY function, and adjust the temperature at 360°F/180°C and set the time for 10 minutes. 2. Press the START/STOP button to activate the function, and allow the oven to preheat. 3. Cut the eggplant into ½-inch slices. 4. Season the eggplant slices with salt on both sides and let them sit for 10 to 15 minutes. 5. Combine the flour, egg, and water in the bowl to make the batter. 6. Mix up the bread crumbs, Parmesan cheese, Italian seasoning blend, and salt in another bowl. 7. Coat the eggplant slices with the batter and then dip them in the breadcrumb mixture. 8. Spray breaded eggplant slices with oil and place them on the roasting pan. 9. Insert the pan inside the oven on position 3, and cook them for 10 minutes. 10. After 8 minutes of cooking time, top the eggplant pieces with about one tablespoon of marinara sauce and fresh mozzarella cheese, then resume cooking them. 11. When the time is up, transfer them to the serving plate or bowl.
Per Serving: Calories 186; Fat 4.67g; Sodium 797mg; Carbs 27.63g; Fiber 6.7g; Sugar 8.61g; Protein 10.47g

Fried Tofu Bites

Prep Time: 35 minutes | Cook Time: 15 minutes | Serves: 4

13 ounces of extra-firm tofu
½ cup Franks hot sauce
½ cup chickpea flour
½ teaspoon garlic powder
Salt to taste

1-½ cup Panko breadcrumbs
¼ cup rice flour
Few tablespoons of water to make a thick batter
Oil spray

1. Select the AIRFRY function, and adjust the temperature at 400°F/200°C and set the time for 15 minutes. 2. Press the START/STOP button to activate the function, and allow the oven to preheat. 3. To press the tofu, drain the tofu and wrap it in paper towels, then lay a heavy item on top. Press the tofu for about 30 minutes. 4. Combine the chickpea flour, garlic powder, and salt in the mixing bowl; mix in a little water until the consistency of the coating is similar to that of the pancake batter. 5. Put the breadcrumbs in another bowl. 6. Cut the pressed tofu into sticks or nugget-sized pieces. 7. Coat the tofu pieces in the rice flour, then in the chickpea flour batter, and lastly, coat them with the breadcrumbs. 8. Arrange the coated tofu pieces in the roasting pan, insert the pan inside the oven on position 3, and then cook them for 15 minutes. 9. Turn the tofu pieces halfway through. 10. You can cook the tofu pieces in batches.
Per Serving: Calories 255; Fat 7.55g; Sodium 432mg; Carbs 33.1g; Fiber 3.6g; Sugar 4.34g; Protein 15.67g

Onion & Sweet Potato Hash

Prep Time: 10 minutes | Cook Time: 30 minutes | Serves: 4

4 sweet potatoes, peel & dice
1 cup mushrooms, sliced
2 tablespoons fresh lemon juice
½ cup bell pepper, chopped
½ cup onion, chopped

½ teaspoon dried rosemary
2 tablespoons canola oil
½ teaspoon dried thyme
Pepper
Salt

1. Select the BAKE function, and adjust the temperature at 360°F/180°C and set the time for 30 minutes. 2. Press the START/STOP button to activate the function, and allow the oven to preheat. 3. Toss the diced sweet potatoes with the remaining ingredients in a bowl and then arrange them in the roasting pan. 4. Insert the pan inside the oven on position 6, and bake the food for 30 minutes, tossing them halfway through cooking. 5. Serve warm.
Per Serving: Calories 184; Fat 7.12g; Sodium 111mg; Carbs 28.67g; Fiber 4.3g; Sugar 6.55g; Protein 2.4g

Pumpkin Pieces

Prep Time: 10 minutes | Cook Time: 15 minutes | Serves: 4

4 cups squash, cut into
pieces
¼ teaspoon dried thyme
¼ teaspoon dried oregano
1 tablespoon parsley,

minced
1 tablespoon canola oil
1 teaspoon garlic, minced
Pepper
Salt

1. Select the BAKE function, and adjust the temperature at 375°F/190°C and set the time for 15 minutes. 2. Press the START/STOP button to activate the function, and allow the oven to preheat. 3. Toss the squash pieces with the remaining ingredients in a bowl and transfer them to the roasting pan. 4. Insert the pan inside the oven on position 6, and bake the food for 30 minutes, stirring them halfway through cooking. 5. Serve warm.
Per Serving: Calories 61; Fat 3.68g; Sodium 50mg; Carbs 6.94g; Fiber 3.2g; Sugar 2.52g; Protein 1.42g

Delicious Cauliflower in Buffalo Sauce

Prep Time: 20 minutes | Cook Time: 15 minutes | Serves: 3

1 medium head cauliflower
2 teaspoons avocado oil
3 tablespoons red hot sauce
2 tablespoons nutritional yeast

1 ½ teaspoons maple syrup
¼ teaspoon sea salt
1 tablespoon cornstarch or
arrowroot starch

1. Select the BAKE function, and adjust the temperature at 365°F/185°C and set the time for 25 minutes. 2. Press the START/STOP button to activate the function, and allow the oven to preheat. 3. Mix the avocado oil, red hot sauce, nutritional yeast, maple syrup, sea salt, and cornstarch in a bowl. 4. Then add the coated cauliflower to the bowl and evenly coat with the mixture. 5. Add the cauliflower to an oven-safe baking dish and place the baking dish onto the air fryer basket. 6. Insert the basket inside the preheated oven on position 6 and bake them for 25 minutes. 7. Serve and enjoy!
Per Serving: Calories 93; Fat 3.45g; Sodium 580mg; Carbs 12.05g; Fiber 2.7g; Sugar 4.24g; Protein 4.7g

Golden Crispy Onion Rings

Prep Time: 5 minutes | Cook Time: 20 minutes | Serves: 3

½ cup almond flour	1 egg, beaten
¾ cup coconut milk	1 tablespoon baking powder
1 big white onion, sliced	1 tablespoon smoked paprika
into rings	Salt and pepper to taste

1. Select the AIRFRY function, and adjust the temperature at 400°F/200°C and set the time for 15 minutes. 2. Press the START/STOP button to activate the function, and allow the oven to preheat. 3. In a medium mixing bowl, add the baking powder, smoked paprika, salt, pepper, and almond flour and mix well. 4. In a separate small bowl, whisk the eggs and coconut milk together. 5. Soak the onion rings in the egg mixture. Then coat them with the flour mixture. 6. Evenly arrange the coated onion rings onto the air fryer basket and insert the basket in the oven on position 3. 7. Cook and turn the onion rings to the other side halfway through cooking. 8. Carefully remove from the oven and transfer to a serving plate. 9. Serve and enjoy!
Per Serving: Calories 231; Fat 18.04g; Sodium 58mg; Carbs 16.09g; Fiber 3.4g; Sugar 8.01g; Protein 5.69g

Parmesan Brussels Sprout

Prep Time: 5 minutes | Cook Time: 16 minutes | Serves: 2

2 tablespoons Parmesan, freshly grated	Caesar dressing for dipping
½ pound Brussels sprouts, thinly sliced	Freshly ground black
1 teaspoon garlic powder	pepper to taste
1 tablespoon extra-virgin olive oil	Kosher salt to taste

1. Select the AIRFRY function, and adjust the temperature at 365°F/185°C and set the time for 16 minutes. 2. Press the START/STOP button to activate the function, and allow the oven to preheat. 3. Add oil, garlic powder, Parmesan, and Brussels sprouts to a large mixing bowl and toss together. 4. Season the mixture with salt and pepper. 5. Evenly arrange the coated Brussels sprouts into the roasting pan and insert the pan in the oven on position 3. 6. Cook until the Brussels sprouts are crispy and golden brown, and toss from time to time while cooking. 7. When the cooking time is up, carefully remove the pan from the oven and transfer the food to a serving plate. 8. Sprinkle with Parmesan cheese. 9. Serve and enjoy!
Per Serving: Calories 102; Fat 3.64g; Sodium 225mg; Carbs 14.01g; Fiber 4.7g; Sugar 2.61g; Protein 6.24g

Stuffed Mushrooms

Prep Time: 5 minutes | Cook Time: 10 minutes | Serves: 3

3 Portobello mushrooms	1 tomato
1 teaspoon garlic	Green pepper
1 medium onion	½ teaspoon sea salt
3 tablespoons grated	¼ teaspoon pepper
mozzarella cheese	1 tablespoon olive oil
2 slices of chopped ham	

1. Select the BAKE function, and adjust the temperature at 400°F/200°C and set the time for 8 minutes. 2. Press the START/STOP button to activate the function, and allow the oven to preheat. 3. Finely chop or dice the tomato, pepper, onion, ham, and garlic and combine them in a bowl. 4. Wash the mushrooms and pat dry. Remove the stems from the mushrooms and drizzle them with oil. 5. Fill the mushroom caps with the tomato-ham mixture. Arrange the mushroom caps in the roasting pan and insert the tray in the oven on position 6. 6. Let them bake in the oven for 8 minutes. 7. When the cooking time is up, carefully remove the tray from the oven. 8. Serve and enjoy!
Per Serving: Calories 134; Fat 8.48g; Sodium 838mg; Carbs 8.94g; Fiber 1.6g; Sugar 4.88g; Protein 6.8g

Broccoli Gratin

Prep Time: 5 minutes | Cook Time: 15 minutes | Serves: 2

⅓ cup fat-free milk
1 tablespoon all-purpose or gluten-free flour
½ tablespoon olive oil
½ teaspoon ground sage
¼ teaspoon kosher salt
⅛ teaspoon freshly ground black pepper
2 cups roughly chopped broccoli florets

6 tablespoons shredded Cheddar cheese
2 tablespoons panko bread crumbs
1 tablespoon grated Parmesan cheese
Olive oil spray

1. Select the BAKE function, and adjust the temperature at 365°F/185°C and set the time for 14 minutes. 2. Press the START/STOP button to activate the function, and allow the oven to preheat. 3. Spray the roasting pan with olive oil. 4. Add milk, flour, salt, sage, pepper, and olive oil to a medium mixing bowl. Whisk well. 5. Add the broccoli to the mixture and then transfer the mixture to the baking dish. 6. Add the bread crumbs, Cheddar cheese, and Parmesan cheese to the baking dish and toss well. 7. Place the baking dish inside the roasting pan and insert the pan inside the oven on position 6. 8. Let them bake for 14 minutes, or until it is golden brown on top. 9. Carefully remove the pan from the oven. 10. Serve and enjoy!

Per Serving: Calories 348; Fat 138.48g; Sodium 1528mg; Carbs 38.01g; Fiber 2.5g; Sugar 10.7g; Protein 19.19g

Breaded Cauliflower Fritters

Prep Time: 10 minutes | Cook Time: 15 minutes | Serves: 8

½ cup chopped parsley
1 cup Italian breadcrumbs
⅓ cup shredded mozzarella cheese
⅓ cup shredded sharp

cheddar cheese
1 egg
2 minced garlic cloves
3 chopped scallions
1 head of cauliflower, cut into florets

1. Select the BAKE function, and adjust the temperature at 400°F/200°C and set the time for 14 minutes. 2. Press the START/STOP button to activate the function, and allow the oven to preheat. 3. Rinse the cauliflower and then pat dry. 4. Transfer to a food processor and pulse until the cauliflower resembles rice. 5. Add the cauliflower rice, parsley, breadcrumbs, mozzarella cheese, cheddar cheese, egg, garlic, and scallions to a mixing bowl. Mix well. 6. Make the mixture into 15 patties and add some extra breadcrumbs as needed. 7. Spray olive oil over the patties and place them onto the roasting pan. 8. Insert the pan inside the oven on position 6 and bake them for 14 minutes.
9. When the patties are cooked, carefully remove the tray from the oven. 10. Serve and enjoy!

Per Serving: Calories 83; Fat 4.35g; Sodium 227mg; Carbs 4.87g; Fiber 1.2g; Sugar 1.37g; Protein 6.58g

Cheese Balls

Prep Time: 10 minutes | Cook Time: 10 minutes | Serves: 12

4 ounces cream cheese
⅓ cup shredded mozzarella cheese
⅓ cup shredded cheddar cheese
2 jalapeños, finely chopped
½ cup bread crumbs

2 eggs
½ cup all-purpose flour
Salt
Pepper
Cooking oil

1. Select the AIRFRY function, and adjust the temperature at 400°F/200°C and set the time for 8 minutes. 2. Press the START/STOP button to activate the function, and allow the oven to preheat. 3. Mix the mozzarella, jalapenos, cheddar, and cream cheese in a medium bowl until well combined. 4. Form the mixture into 1-inch thick balls. Place the balls into a baking sheet and then freeze in the freezer for about 15 minutes. 5. Spray cooking spray over the air fryer basket. 6. Add the breadcrumbs to a bowl, and in another bowl, beat the eggs. 7. In the third bowl, add flour, pepper, and salt and whisk well. 8. Dip the frozen balls first in the flour, then in the eggs, and coat with the breadcrumbs, pressing to coat well. 9. Place the balls onto the basket and insert the basket inside the oven on position 3. 10. Cook and carefully turn the cheese balls halfway through. 11. Carefully remove from the oven. 12. Serve and enjoy!

Per Serving: Calories 91; Fat 4.93g; Sodium 165mg; Carbs 6.98g; Fiber 0.4g; Sugar 1.56g; Protein 4.8g

Chapter 4 Fish and Seafood Recipes

Vegetable Tilapia Tacos

Prep Time: 30 minutes | Cook Time: 30 minutes | Serves: 12

Fish Taco

24 small white corn tortillas	1 teaspoon salt
1½-pound tilapia	¼ teaspoon black pepper
½ teaspoon ground cumin	1 tablespoon olive oil
½ teaspoon cayenne pepper	1 tablespoon butter

Taco Toppings

½ small purple cabbage	½ bunch cilantro, longer stems removed
2 medium avocados, sliced	4 ounces cotija cheese, grated
½ red onion, diced	1 lime, cut into 8 wedges, to serve

Taco Sauce

½ cup sour cream	from 1 medium lime
⅓ cup mayonnaise	1 teaspoon garlic powder
2 tablespoons lime juice	1 teaspoon Sriracha sauce or to taste

1. Select the BAKE function, and adjust the temperature at 375°F/190°C and set the time for 25 minutes. 2. Press the START/STOP button to activate the function, and allow the oven to preheat. 3. Line the roasting pan with parchment. 4. Add ½ teaspoon of cumin, ½ teaspoon of cayenne pepper, one teaspoon of salt, and ¼ teaspoon of black pepper to a small bowl and mix them well. Evenly sprinkle the seasoning mix over both sides of the tilapia. 5. Arrange the fish on the pan, drizzle with olive oil and dot each piece with butter. 6. Place the pan in the oven on position 6. 7. To brown the edges, turn the dial to broil and broil the fish for 3 to 5 minutes at the end of the baking time, if desired. 8. Mix all the taco sauce ingredients in a bowl until well blended. 9. Quickly toast the corn tortillas in a dry skillet over medium-high heat. 10. Arrange the fish pieces on the tortillas, add the remaining ingredients, and finish with a generous sprinkle of cotija cheese and the awesome taco sauce!
Per Serving: Calories 255; Fat 13.86g; Sodium 467mg; Carbs 19g; Fiber 4.7g; Sugar 2.55g; Protein 16.25g

Chili Tilapia

Prep Time: 5 minutes | Cook Time: 10 minutes | Serves: 2

12 ounces tilapia fillets (6 to 8 ounces each)	½ teaspoon sea salt
2 teaspoons chili powder	¼ teaspoon ground black pepper
1 teaspoon cumin	Zest from 1 lime
1 teaspoon garlic powder	Juice of ½ lime
½ teaspoon oregano	

1. Select the ROAST function, and adjust the temperature at 350°F/175°C and set the time for 10 minutes. 2. Press the START/STOP button to activate the function, and allow the oven to preheat. 3. Use a paper towel to pat dry the tilapia fillets. 4. Combine all the ingredients except for the fish and the lime juice in the bowl. 5. Coat the fish with the spice mix on all sides. 6. Place the fish in the roasting pan, insert the pan inside the oven on position 2, and then roast the food for 10 minutes. 7. When done, transfer the fish to the serving plate.
Per Serving: Calories 191; Fat 3.57g; Sodium 751mg; Carbs 6.42g; Fiber 1.5g; Sugar 1.11g; Protein 35.24g

Glazed Salmon Fillets

Prep Time: 35 minutes | Cook Time: 10 minutes | Serves: 4

⅓ cup maple syrup	½ teaspoon coarsely ground black pepper
3 tablespoons low-sodium soy sauce	1 pound salmon fillets
½ teaspoon garlic powder	

1. Select the ROAST function, and adjust the temperature at 350°F/175°C and set the time for 10 minutes. 2. Press the START/STOP button to activate the function, and allow the oven to preheat. 3. Add the maple syrup, soy sauce, garlic powder, and pepper to a large Ziploc bag, seal the bag and shake to make sure everything gets combined. 4. Open the bag and add the salmon fillets. Place the bag in the fridge and marinate the fillets for 30 minutes. 5. Place the marinated salmon fillets in the roasting pan. 6. Insert the pan inside the oven on position 6, and then roast the for 10 minutes. 7. When done, serve.
Per Serving: Calories 249; Fat 8.19g; Sodium 878mg; Carbs 18.51g; Fiber 0.2g; Sugar 15.78g; Protein 24.27g

Crab Shrimp Roll

Prep Time: 20 minutes | Cook Time: 15 minutes | Serves: 12

2 tablespoons butter
½ cup onion, finely diced
¼ cup red bell pepper, finely diced
¼ cup green bell pepper, finely diced
1-pound lump crabmeat
½ cup panko crumbs
12 Ritz crackers, crushed

1 teaspoon Old Bay seasoning
½ teaspoon lemon zest
¼ teaspoon cayenne pepper
½ cup mayonnaise
1 large egg
Salt and pepper
24 jumbo or large shrimp
2 tablespoons butter, melted

1. Select the ROAST function, and adjust the temperature at 350°F/175°C and set the time for 15 minutes. 2. Press the START/STOP button to activate the function, and allow the oven to preheat. 3. Melt the butter in a nonstick pan over medium-high heat. 4. Add the onion, red bell pepper, and green bell pepper to the skillet, and sauté them for 3 minutes or until soft. Let them cool after cooking. 5. Pick through the crabmeat and remove any shell. Place the crab in a medium bowl, add the panko crumbs, Ritz crackers, Old Bay seasoning, lemon zest, cayenne pepper, mayonnaise, and egg and then gently stir them to mix. 6. Season the mixture with salt and pepper and place in the refrigerator. 7. Peel the shrimp, leaving the tails on. Cut through the backside of each shrimp, like you would to devein it, but cut more deeply, almost all the way through. Remove and discard the veins. 8. Place the shrimp on the baking pan, butterflied side down, pressing to flatten. 9. Shape about one heaping tablespoon of crab mixture into a ball and place on top of a shrimp, pressing the tail into the top to secure. Do the same with the remaining mixture and shrimps. 10. Place them in the roasting pan, drizzle the melted butter over the shrimp. 11. Insert the pan inside the oven on position 2, and roast them for 15 minutes. 12. When done, serve and enjoy.
Per Serving: Calories 142; Fat 9.87g; Sodium 386mg; Carbs 5.06g; Fiber 0.8g; Sugar 1.02g; Protein 8.35g

Rosemary Baked Salmon

Prep Time: 15 minutes | Cook Time: 25 minutes | Serves: 6

2 pounds' side of salmon, boneless
5 sprigs of fresh rosemary
2 small lemons, divided
2 tablespoons extra virgin olive oil
1 teaspoon kosher salt

¼ teaspoon ground black pepper
4 cloves garlic, peeled and roughly chopped

1. Select the BAKE function, and adjust the temperature at 375°F/190°C and set the time for 20 minutes. 2. Press the START/STOP button to activate the function, and allow the oven to preheat. 3. Line the roasting pan with a piece of aluminum foil. 4. Lightly coat the foil with baking spray, and then arrange two sprigs of the rosemary down the middle. 5. Cut one of the lemons into thin slices and arrange half the pieces down the middle with the rosemary. Place the salmon on top. 6. Drizzle the salmon with olive oil and season with salt and pepper. Rub to coat, and then scatter the garlic cloves over the top. 7. Place the remaining rosemary and lemon slices on top of the salmon. Juice the second lemon, then pour the juice over the top. 8. Fold the sides of the aluminum foil up and over the top of the salmon until it's completely enclosed. Leave a little room inside the foil for air to circulate. 9. Insert the pan inside the oven on position 6, and then bake the food for 20 minutes. 10. When the time is up, the salmon should be almost completely cooked through at the thickest part. 11. Then, broil the salmon at LOW for 3 minutes until the top of the salmon and the garlic are slightly golden, and the fish is cooked through. 12. Serve warm.
Per Serving: Calories 208; Fat 7.83g; Sodium 504mg; Carbs 2.12g; Fiber 0.3g; Sugar 0.42g; Protein 30.71g

Breaded Cod Fillets

Prep Time: 15 minutes | Cook Time: 15 minutes | Serves: 2

1 pound cod fillets	¼ teaspoon onion powder
1 cup panko bread crumbs	¼ teaspoon fresh parsley,
1 large egg beaten	chopped
¼ teaspoon garlic salt	Olive oil spray

1. Select the BAKE function, and adjust the temperature at 400°F/200°C and set the time for 15 minutes. 2. Press the START/STOP button to activate the function, and allow the oven to preheat. 3. Add the panko bread crumbs to a bowl, and in another bowl, mix the egg with the garlic salt, onion powder, and parsley. 4. Dip the cod fillets into the egg mix and then into the panko bread crumbs, covering them lightly in bread crumbs. 5. Spray each piece of cod with cooking spray and arrange the cod fillets on the roasting pan, then slide the pan into the position 6. 6. Bake the fillets for 15 minutes. 7. You can serve when the cod filets are golden brown and flake easily.

Per Serving: Calories 232; Fat 3.77g; Sodium 777mg; Carbs 9.32g; Fiber 0.5g; Sugar 1.06g; Protein 37.59g

Cajun Salmon Fillet

Prep Time: 5 minutes | Cook Time: 20 minutes | Serves: 4

2 to 4 pounds salmon fillet	juice
1 tablespoon fresh lemon	2 tablespoons Cajun seasoning blend

1. Select the ROAST function, and adjust the temperature at 350°F/175°C and set the time for 20 minutes. 2. Press the START/STOP button to activate the function, and allow the oven to preheat. 3. Arrange the salmon fillets on the roasting pan; drizzle the fillets with the lemon juice, and season with the Cajun blend. 4. Insert the pan inside the oven on position 6, and then roast the food for 20 minutes. 5. When cooked, serve warm.

Per Serving: Calories 287; Fat 8.56g; Sodium 421mg; Carbs 2.74g; Fiber 0.6g; Sugar 0.56g; Protein 45.88g

Panko-Crusted Shrimp

Prep Time: 15 minutes | Cook Time: 15 minutes | Serves: 4

1 pound uncooked large shrimp (25 to 30), thawed if frozen	2 large eggs
½ cup all-purpose flour	1½ cups panko breadcrumbs
1 teaspoon seasoning salt	Cooking spray

1. Select the AIRFRY function, and adjust the temperature at 350°F/175°C and set the time for 15 minutes. 2. Press the START/STOP button to activate the function, and allow the oven to preheat. 3. Peel and devein the shrimp (optional) and set the shrimp aside for later use. 4. In a mixing bowl, mix up the all-purpose flour and seasoning salt in a shallow dish or bowl. 5. Lightly beat the eggs in a second bowl and add the panko breadcrumbs in a third bowl. 6. Dip the shrimp in the flour mixture and then dip in the egg. Let the excess egg drip back into the bowl; lastly, coat the shrimp entirely in the panko. 7. Place the coated shrimp onto the air fryer basket, insert the basket inside the oven on position 3, and then cook them for 15 minutes. 8. When the shrimp has cooked, let it cool for 5 minutes before serving.

Per Serving: Calories 325; Fat 5.7g; Sodium 1524mg; Carbs 42.41g; Fiber 2.2g; Sugar 2.6g; Protein 23.8g

Pineapple Roasted Fish

Prep Time: 20 minutes | Cook Time: 15 minutes | Serves: 6

10 ounces fish filet, sliced into ¼-inch thin slices

2 tablespoons potato starch mixed with 2 tablespoons plain flour

⅓ cup cooking oil

4 shallots, peeled and halved

¼ cup green bell pepper, diced

For the sweet and sour sauce:

5 tablespoons tomato sauce

3 tablespoons chili sauce

3 tablespoons plum sauce

¼ cup red bell pepper, diced

¼ cup yellow bell pepper, diced

1 tomato, cut into wedges

2 ounces canned pineapple, diced

1 tablespoon lemon juice

2 tablespoons brown sugar

½ teaspoon salt or to taste

1. Select the ROAST function, and adjust the temperature at 400°F/200°C and set the time for 10 minutes. 2. Press the START/STOP button to activate the function, and allow the oven to preheat. 3. Heat all the sauce ingredients in a saucepan over medium-high heat, and bring to a gentle boil. Turn off the heat and set the sauce aside for later use. 4. Coat the fish slices thoroughly in the flour-starch mixture. Shake off the excess and discard. Set aside. 5. Place the fish on the roasting pan and sprinkle oil over the top. 6. Insert the pan inside the oven on position 6, and then roast for 10 minutes until the fish is light brown. 7. Add the sauce on top of the fish and toss. If the sauce is too thick, add 2 to 3 tablespoons of water, and the sauce should still be slightly thick and sticky, not watery. 8. Roast the food for 5 minutes longer. Toss the fish once done to coat it in the sauce thoroughly.

Per Serving: Calories 314; Fat 19.86g; Sodium 591mg; Carbs 23.72g; Fiber 2.4g; Sugar 15.27g; Protein 10.5g

Shrimp-Rice Stuffed Peppers

Prep Time: 10 minutes | Cook Time: 50 minutes | Serves: 10

6 cups cooked rice

1½ tablespoon olive oil

½ stick butter

2 pounds of medium-sized shrimp (peeled and deveined)

1½ teaspoons Creole seasoning

1 large yellow onion, chopped

1 yellow bell pepper, chopped

2 cloves garlic, chopped

15 ounces can of diced tomatoes

8 ounces can tomato sauce

10 ounces can cream of mushroom

6 red bell peppers

1–2 cups of water

1½ cups shredded cheese

Fresh chopped parsley

1. Select the AIRFRY function, and adjust the temperature at 350°F/175°C and set the time for 25 minutes. 2. Press the START/STOP button to activate the function, and allow the oven to preheat. 3. Boil a pot of water. 4. Cut the whole red bell peppers in half and remove their ribs and seeds; rinse the peppers and use the paper towel to pat them dry. 5. Add the peppers to the boiling water and wait for 5 minutes to parboil them, and then arrange them in the roasting pan. 6. Mix the shrimps with the Creole seasoning. 7. Heat the olive oil and butter in a skillet over medium-high heat; add the shrimps and sauté them for 3 to 5 minutes until cooked through, then transfer them to a bowl. 8. Still in the skillet, add a little more oil, the onion, chopped green bell peppers, garlic, and Creole seasoning, and sauté them for 10 minutes or until the onions are transparent. 9. Lower the heat to medium-low and sauté the diced tomatoes, tomato sauce, and cream of mushroom. 10. Add the shrimps back to the pot or skillet and stir in the cooked rice. 11. When cooked, apportion the shrimp-rice mixture between the half peppers. 12. Pour about ½ cup of water in the pan and then cover the pan with foil. 13. Place the dish in the oven on position 3 and let it cook. 14. Once done, carefully remove the foil and top the mixture with a little shredded cheese and fresh parsley.

Per Serving: Calories 419; Fat 12.37g; Sodium 762mg; Carbs 56.52g; Fiber 7.6g; Sugar 4.71g; Protein 24.5g

Flavorful Tilapia Fillets

Prep Time: 5 minutes | Cook Time: 20 minutes | Serves: 2

12 ounces tilapia fillets or other white fish (2 filets: 6 ounces each)
½ teaspoon garlic powder
½ teaspoon lemon-pepper seasoning
½ teaspoon onion powder (optional)
Kosher salt or sea salt, to taste

Fresh cracked black pepper, to taste
Fresh chopped parsley for garnish
Lemon wedges, to serve

1. Select the AIRFRY function, and adjust the temperature at 350°F/175°C and set the time for 20 minutes. 2. Press the START/STOP button to activate the function, and allow the oven to preheat. 3. Rinse the tilapia fillets and then use the paper towel to dry them; coat them with olive oil and season with garlic powder, lemon-pepper seasoning, onion powder (optional), salt, and black pepper on both sides. 4. Place the fish in the roasting pan in a single layer, insert the pan inside the oven on position 3, and then cook the fish for 20 minutes. 5. When cooked, serve and enjoy with the lemon wedges.
Per Serving: Calories 306; Fat 16.4g; Sodium 258mg; Carbs 5.49g; Fiber 1.6g; Sugar 1.54g; Protein 33g

Cheese Fillets

Prep Time: 10 minutes | Cook Time: 15 minutes | Serves: 4

1 pound salmon or halibut fillet
½ cup butter

2 ½ tablespoons mayonnaise
2 ½ tablespoons lemon juice
¾ cup Parmesan cheese, grated

1. Select the ROAST function, and adjust the temperature at 375°F/190°C and set the time for 12 minutes. 2. Press the START/STOP button to activate the function, and allow the oven to preheat. 3. Spritz the fillets with cooking spray. 4. Mix the butter, mayonnaise, and lemon juice in the bowl; stir in the grated Parmesan cheese. 5. Coat the fillets with the mixture and place the fillets on the roasting pan. 6. Insert the pan inside the oven on position 6, and then roast the food for 12 minutes. 7. Serve hot.
Per Serving: Calories 488; Fat 39.37g; Sodium 1084mg; Carbs 3.57g; Fiber 0.1g; Sugar 0.35g; Protein 29.56g

Red Snapper with Lemon Slices

Prep Time: 10 minutes | Cook Time: 10 minutes | Serves: 4

1 teaspoon olive oil
1½ teaspoons black pepper
¼ teaspoon garlic powder
¼ teaspoon thyme
⅛ teaspoon cayenne pepper

4 (4-ounce) red snapper fillets, skin on
4 thin slices of lemon
Cooking spray

1. Select the BAKE function, and adjust the temperature at 390°F/195°C and set the time for 10 minutes. 2. Press the START/STOP button to activate the function, and allow the oven to preheat. 3. Grease the roasting pan with cooking spray. 4. Mix up the olive oil, black pepper, garlic powder, thyme, and cayenne pepper in a small bowl. 5. Coat the fillets with the mixture on all sides. 6. Arrange the fillets, skin-side down, to the pan, and top each fillet with a slice of lemon. 7. Insert the pan inside the oven on position 6 and bake the food for 10 minutes, turning them over halfway through. 8. When done, remove the lemon slices and let the fillets cool for 5 minutes before serving.
Per Serving: Calories 33; Fat 1.21g; Sodium 5mg; Carbs 5.4g; Fiber 0.8g; Sugar 0.38g; Protein 0.69g

Cornmeal-Crusted Catfish Fillets

Prep Time: 15 minutes | Cook Time: 10 minutes | Serves: 4

1½ teaspoons Creole seasoning
½ cup buttermilk
½ to ¾ pound catfish fillets cut into 2-inch strips if the fillets are large
½ cup all-purpose flour

⅓ cup cornmeal
1 teaspoon salt
½ teaspoon ground black pepper
2 tablespoons vegetable oil
Lemon wedges, for serving
Tartar sauce, for serving

1. Select the AIRFRY function, and adjust the temperature at 400°F/200°C and set the time for 10 minutes. 2. Press the START/STOP button to activate the function, and allow the oven to preheat. 3. Toss the Creole seasoning and buttermilk in a small mixing dish; evenly coat the catfish fillets with the mixture. 4. Combine the flour, cornmeal, salt, and black pepper in another bowl. 5. Coat the fillets with the cornmeal mixture and then transfer the fillets to a plate. 6. Drizzle the vegetable oil over the fillets and turn to coat evenly. 7. Place the fillets on the air fryer basket and insert the basket inside the oven on position 3, then cook them for 10 minutes. 8. When done, serve and enjoy.
Per Serving: Calories 320; Fat 17.19g; Sodium 749mg; Carbs 25.66g; Fiber 1.2g; Sugar 2.42g; Protein 14.71g

Breaded Flounder Fillets

Prep Time: 5 minutes | Cook Time: 15 minutes | Serves: 4

1 cup dry breadcrumbs
¼ cup vegetable oil
4 flounder fillets

1 egg, beaten
1 lemon, sliced

1. Select the AIRFRY function, and adjust the temperature at 350°F/175°C and set the time for 15 minutes. 2. Press the START/STOP button to activate the function, and allow the oven to preheat. 3. Mix the breadcrumbs and vegetable oil in a bowl until the mixture becomes loose and crumbly. 4. Beat the egg in another bowl. 5. Dip the fillets into the egg; shake off any excess. Then dip the fillets into the breadcrumb mixture; coat evenly and thoroughly. 6. Place the fillets on the air fryer basket, insert the basket inside the oven on position, and then air-fry them for 15 minutes. 7. Serve the fillets with the sauce of your choice.
Per Serving: Calories 506; Fat 32.79g; Sodium 640mg; Carbs 28.17g; Fiber 6.4g; Sugar 2.82g; Protein 25.44g

Lemon Shrimp

Prep Time: 5 minutes | Cook Time: 15 minutes | Serves: 2

1 tablespoon olive oil
1 lemon, juiced
1 teaspoon lemon pepper
¼ teaspoon paprika

¼ teaspoon garlic powder
12 ounces uncooked medium shrimp, peeled and deveined
1 lemon, sliced

1. Select the AIRFRY function, and adjust the temperature at 350°F/175°C and set the time for 15 minutes. 2. Press the START/STOP button to activate the function, and allow the oven to preheat. 3. Mix the olive oil, lemon juice, lemon pepper, paprika, and garlic powder in a bowl. 4. Coat the shrimps with the paprika mixture. 5. Place the coated shrimp onto the roasting pan, insert the pan inside the oven on position 3, and then cook the food for 15 minutes. 6. Let the shrimps cool for 5 minutes after cooking, and then serve with the lemon slices.
Per Serving: Calories 202; Fat 8.67g; Sodium 965mg; Carbs 7.44g; Fiber 0.6g; Sugar 2.4g; Protein 23.88g

Cod Fillets

Prep Time: 10 minutes | Cook Time: 12 minutes | Serves: 4

4 cod fillets	½ cup milk
¼ teaspoon fine sea salt	4 garlic cloves, minced
1 teaspoon cayenne pepper	1 pepper, chopped
¼ teaspoon ground black pepper, or more to taste	1 teaspoon dried basil
	½ teaspoon dried oregano
½ cup fresh parsley, coarsely chopped	Cooking spray

1. Select the AIRFRY function, and adjust the temperature at 375°F/190°C and set the time for 12 minutes. 2. Press the START/STOP button to activate the function, and allow the oven to preheat. 3. Lightly grease the air fryer basket with cooking spray. 4. Season the fillets with salt, cayenne pepper, and black pepper. 5. Pulse the remaining ingredients in a food processor and transfer the mixture to a bowl. 6. Coat the fillets with the mixture, and then place them in the basket. 7. Insert the basket inside the oven on position 3, and then air-fry the food for 12 minutes. 8. When the fillets are flaky, serve.

Per Serving: Calories 111; Fat 1.66g; Sodium 515mg; Carbs 3.98g; Fiber 0.7g; Sugar 1.84g; Protein 19.71g

Cornmeal Squid

Prep Time: 10 minutes | Cook Time: 15 minutes | Serves: 6

½ teaspoon salt	½ cup semolina flour
½ teaspoon Old bay seasoning	1 to 2 pinches of pepper
	6 cup olive oil
⅓ cup plain cornmeal	1½ pounds baby squid, rinsed

1. Select the AIRFRY function, and adjust the temperature at 345°F/175°C and set the time for 15 minutes. 2. Press the START/STOP button to activate the function, and allow the oven to preheat. 3. Slice the tentacles of the squid, keeping just ¼-inch of the hood in one piece. 4. In the bowl, mix up the Old bay seasoning, cornmeal, flours, salt, and 1 to 2 pinches of pepper. 5. Dredge squid pieces into the flour mixture and then arrange them into the air fryer basket; liberally spray them with the olive oil. 6. Insert the basket inside the oven on position 3, and then cook the food for 15 minutes until the coating turns a golden brown. 7. Serve warm.

Per Serving: Calories 1418; Fat 114.39g; Sodium 458mg; Carbs 92.73g; Fiber 2.9g; Sugar 47.63g; Protein 8.48g

Breaded Fish Fingers

Prep Time: 10 minutes | Cook Time: 15 minutes | Serves: 2

1 pound of fish fillets	2 eggs
½ cup all-purpose flour	1 cup dried breadcrumbs
1 teaspoon salt, divided	
½ teaspoon ground black pepper divided	

1. Select the AIRFRY function, and adjust the temperature at 400°F/200°C and set the time for 15 minutes. 2. Press the START/STOP button to activate the function, and allow the oven to preheat. 3. Season the fish fillets with salt and let them marinate for 20 to 30 minutes. 4. Mix the flour with salt and pepper in a bowl; in the second bowl, beat the eggs, and in the third bowl, add the dried breadcrumbs. 5. Dredge the fillets in the flour, dip them in egg and then thoroughly coat them with breadcrumbs. 6. Place the coated fillets in the air fryer basket, and then insert the basket inside the oven on position 3. 7. After 10 minutes of cooking time, flip the fillets and then resume cooking them in the oven. 8. Serve warm.

Per Serving: Calories 666; Fat 32.03g; Sodium 1500mg; Carbs 34.57g; Fiber 1.5g; Sugar 2.3g; Protein 55.88

Broiled Lobster Tail

Prep Time: 10 minutes | Cook Time: 8 minutes | Serves: 4

6 ounces of lobster tails,
shell cut from the top
⅛ teaspoon salt
⅛ teaspoon black pepper

⅛ teaspoon paprika
1 tablespoon butter
½ lemon, cut into wedges
Chopped parsley for garnish

1. Place the processed lobster tails in the roasting pan. 2. In the bowl, mix up the remaining ingredients and then pour over the lobster tails. 3. Broil the lobster tails at High for 8 minutes. 4. Serve warm after cooking.
Per Serving: Calories 60; Fat 3.23g; Sodium 280mg; Carbs 0.52g; Fiber 0.1g; Sugar 0.16g; Protein 7.1g

Garlic Salmon

Prep Time: 10 minutes | Cook Time: 10 minutes | Serves: 3

2 salmon fillets
½ teaspoon lemon pepper
½ teaspoon garlic powder
Salt and pepper to taste

⅓ cup soy sauce
⅓ cup sugar
1 tablespoon olive oil

1. Select the AIRFRY function, and adjust the temperature at 350°F/175°C and set the time for 10 minutes. 2. Press the START/STOP button to activate the function, and allow the oven to preheat. 3. Sprinkle the salmon fillets with garlic powder, lemon powder, salt, and pepper. 4. Add a third cup of water to a shallow bowl and combine the olive oil, soy sauce, and sugar; immerse in the salmon fillets sauce. 5. Cover the fillets with cling film and marinate them in the refrigerator for at least 1 hour. 6. Place the fillets in the air fryer basket, insert the basket inside the oven on position 3, and then cook them for 10 minutes. 7. You can cook the fillets longer until they are tender. 8. Serve immediately.
Per Serving: Calories 331; Fat 14.64g; Sodium 491mg; Carbs 19.92g; Fiber 0.9g; Sugar 16.97g; Protein 29.01g

Jumbo Lump Crab Cakes

Prep Time: 10 minutes | Cook Time: 10 minutes | Serves: 4

8 ounces jumbo lump
crabmeat
1 tablespoon Old Bay
Seasoning
⅓ cup bread crumbs
¼ cup diced red bell pepper

¼ cup chopped green bell pepper
1 egg
¼ cup mayonnaise
Juice of ½ lemon
1 teaspoon flour
Cooking oil

1. Select the BAKE function, and adjust the temperature at 355°F/180°C and set the time for 10 minutes. 2. Press the START/STOP button to activate the function, and allow the oven to preheat. 3. In a large mixing bowl, mix the crabmeat, Old Bay Seasoning, bread crumbs, red bell pepper, green bell pepper, egg, mayonnaise, and lemon juice. 4. Form the mixture into four patties; sprinkle each cake with ¼ teaspoon of flour. 5. Arrange the cakes in the roasting pan and then coat them with the cooking oil. 6. Insert the pan inside the oven on position 6 and bake the cakes for 10 minutes. 7. Serve warm.
Per Serving: Calories 142; Fat 11.24g; Sodium 573mg; Carbs 7.11g; Fiber 1.9g; Sugar 0.9g; Protein 4.18g

Dijon Tuna Cakes

Prep Time: 10 minutes | Cook Time: 12 minutes | Serves: 4

2 (6-ounce) cans of water-packed plain tuna
2 teaspoons Dijon mustard
½ cup breadcrumbs
1 tablespoon fresh lime juice
2 tablespoons fresh parsley, chopped

1 egg
3 tablespoons canola oil
Salt and ground black pepper to taste

1. Select the BAKE function, and adjust the temperature at 355°F/180°C and set the time for 12 minutes. 2. Press the START/STOP button to activate the function, and allow the oven to preheat. 3. Drain most of the liquid from the canned tuna. 4. Mix the drained tunas with the mustard, crumbs, lemon juice, parsley, and hot sauce till well combined. 5. Add a little canola oil if it seems too dry. Add egg and salt and stir them to combine. 6. Form the patties from the tuna mixture and then let the cakes sit in the refrigerator for about 2 hours. 7. Arrange the patties in the roasting pan, insert the pan inside the oven, and then bake them for 12 minutes. 8. Serve warm.

Per Serving: Calories 223; Fat 14.16g; Sodium 259mg; Carbs 11.62g; Fiber 1g; Sugar 1.68g; Protein 12.7g

Fried Mackerel Fillets

Prep Time: 10 minutes | Cook Time: 10 minutes | Serves: 4

2 mackerel fillets
2 tablespoons red chili flakes

2 teaspoons garlic, minced
1 teaspoon lemon juice

1. Select the AIRFRY function, and adjust the temperature at 350°F/175°C and set the time for 10 minutes. 2. Press the START/STOP button to activate the function, and allow the oven to preheat. 3. Mix the mackerel fillets with the red chili flakes, minced garlic, and a drizzle of lemon juice. 4. Allow them to sit for 5 minutes. 5. Place the fillets in the air fryer basket, insert the basket inside the oven, and then cook them. 6. After 5 minutes of cooking time, flip the fillets and allow cooking on the other side for another 5 minutes. 7. Plate the fillets, making sure to spoon any remaining juice over them before serving.

Per Serving: Calories 211; Fat 3.98g; Sodium 343mg; Carbs 0.82g; Fiber 0g; Sugar 0.05g; Protein 40.3g

Breadcrumb-Crusted Flounder Fillets

Prep Time: 10 minutes | Cook Time: 12 minutes | Serves: 3

1 egg
1 cup dry breadcrumbs
¼ cup vegetable oil

3 (6 ounces) flounder fillets
1 lemon, sliced

1. Select the AIRFRY function, and adjust the temperature at 350°F/175°C and set the time for 12 minutes. 2. Press the START/STOP button to activate the function, and allow the oven to preheat. 3. Crack the egg into a small bowl and beat well. 4. Mix the breadcrumbs and oil in another bowl until a crumbly mixture is formed. 5. Dip flounder fillets into the beaten egg and then coat with the breadcrumb mixture. 6. Arrange the flounder fillets to the air fryer basket, and then insert the basket inside the oven on position 3 to cook them better. 7. Serve hot.

Per Serving: Calories 437; Fat 31.72g; Sodium 337mg; Carbs 25.43g; Fiber 6g; Sugar 17.47g; Protein 16.35g

Fried Crusted Chicken

Prep Time: 10 minutes | Cook Time: 40 minutes | Serves: 6

2 cups buttermilk
2 tablespoons salt
1 teaspoon sugar
½ teaspoon ground black pepper

6 chicken legs
6 chicken thighs
1 cup flour
6 eggs
6 cups flaked corn cereal, crushed

1. Select the BAKE function, and adjust the temperature at 375°F/190°C and set the time for 40 minutes. 2. Press the START/STOP button to activate the function, and allow the oven to preheat. 3. Add salt, black pepper, buttermilk, and sugar and mix together. Then add the chicken thighs and legs to soak. 4. Whisk the eggs in a shallow baking dish. 5. In a second dish, add the flour. 6. Prepare a third dish with flaked corn cereal. 7. Drain the chicken thighs and legs and get rid of any excess buttermilk. 8. Then dredge the chicken pieces into the flour to coat. Add in the egg mixture. Finally, put the chicken pieces in the corn cereal, pressing them to coat well. 9. Arrange the chicken legs and chicken thighs onto the roasting pan, insert the pan inside the oven on position 6, and then bake the food for 40 minutes. 10. Serve and enjoy!
Per Serving: Calories 800; Fat 27.01g; Sodium 2760mg; Carbs 82.49g; Fiber 6.7g; Sugar 5.07g; Protein 55.92g

Chicken and Veggies Pot Pie

Prep Time: 20 minutes | Cook Time: 30 minutes | Serves: 8

4 tablespoons unsalted butter
1-pound boneless skinless chicken breast, cut into small bite-size pieces
1 cup sliced carrots
½ cup sliced celery
½ cup chopped yellow onion
1¼ teaspoons salt
½ teaspoon garlic powder
½ teaspoon dried thyme leaves
¼ teaspoon ground black pepper

¼ cup all-purpose flour
½ cup heavy cream
1 cup chicken broth
½ cup frozen peas
2 tablespoons freshly minced flat-leaf parsley
2 unbaked pie crusts, 1 top and 1 bottom

1. Select the BAKE function, and adjust the temperature at 335°F/170°C and set the time for 30 minutes. 2. Press the START/STOP button to activate the function, and allow the oven to preheat. 3. Add the butter to a large skillet, and heat it over medium heat. Once the butter is just about to bubble, add the carrots, salt, celery, garlic powder, pepper, thyme leaves, chicken, and onion. Cook in the skillet for about 8 to 10 minutes, stirring them often. 4. Stir in flour and make sure no flour remains. Then add cream and then the chicken broth. Stir and cook for 3 to 4 minutes, or until the cooking liquid is thick and bubbling. 5. Remove it from heat and add the parsley and peas. Stir well and allow it to cool for the pie fillings, about 3 to 4 minutes. 6. In a 9-inch pie plate, add 1 pie crust and then fill in the pie filling. Add the second pie crust. Then seal the edges of the pie crust together and cut 3 to 4 slits in the top crust as a vent. 7. Set the oven on the Bake function, and adjust the temperature to 335°F/170°C and time to 30 minutes. 8. Transfer the plate onto the roasting pan, insert the pan inside the oven on position 6, and then bake the pie for 30 minutes. 9. When cooked, remove the pan from the oven. Allow it to cool for about 15 to 30 minutes. 10. Slice and serve!
Per Serving: Calories 405; Fat 23.03g; Sodium 817mg; Carbs 25.26g; Fiber 1.4g; Sugar 0.65g; Protein 23.16g

Herbed Turkey Roast

Prep Time: 15 minutes | Cook Time: 2 hours 30 minutes | Serves: 12

1(12 to 14 pounds) whole turkey, thawed if frozen
3 tablespoons extra-virgin olive oil
1 teaspoon salt
½ teaspoon freshly ground black pepper
3 sprigs of fresh rosemary
Cranberry gravy
2 cups sweetened dried cranberries
1 cup water
¼ cup sugar

2 sprigs of fresh thyme
2 sprigs of fresh sage
2 sprigs of fresh oregano
1 lemon, halved
2 carrots, halved
4 celery stalks, halved
4 cups chicken broth
4 cups water

2 teaspoons fresh sage leaves, chopped
¾ cup all-purpose flour
¾ cup butter
4 cups chicken broth

1. Select the ROAST function, and adjust the temperature at 335°F/170°C and set the time for 2 hours and 30 minutes. 2. Press the START/STOP button to activate the function, and allow the oven to preheat. 3. Rinse both inside and out of the turkey and brush with oil. 4. Add salt and pepper to season, pressing to coat. 5. Fill in the cavity of the turkey with 2 rosemary sprigs, lemon halves, 1 oregano sprig, 1 sage sprig, and 1 oregano sprig. 6. Place the turkey onto the roasting pan. 7. Arrange celery, carrots, and the rest herbs on the bottom of the pan around the turkey. Pour 4 cups of broth and 4 cups of water over the herbs and vegetables. 8. Roast the food for 2 hours 30 minutes until the internal temperature of the turkey reaches 165°F/74°C, basting the broth over the chicken every 30 minutes. 9. Carefully remove the pan from the oven and let it cool for 15 minutes. Reserve the chicken broth mixture and discard the vegetables. 10. Add 1 cup of water, sugar, and cranberries to a suitable saucepan. Simmer until the cranberries are tender, about 20 minutes. 11. Then let it cool for about 5 minutes. 12. Add 2 teaspoons of sage and the cranberry mixture to a blender and blend until smooth. Set it aside for later use. 13. Add the flour and butter to a medium and heavy saucepan. Cook over medium heat for about 3 to 4 minutes and stir it often until a roux has been formed. Then add 4 cups of broth, the cranberry puree, and the reserved broth. Bring to a boil over high heat. 14. Simmer and stir to thicken the sauce. 15. Enjoy!
Per Serving: Calories 351; Fat 28.15g; Sodium 870mg; Carbs 16.63g; Fiber 1g; Sugar 8.47g; Protein 8.49g

Herb Chicken Thighs

Prep Time: 20 minutes | Cook Time: 50 minutes | Serves: 8

3 pounds of bone-in chicken thighs
2 tablespoons avocado oil
¼ cup fresh lemon juice
1 teaspoon lemon zest
1½ tablespoons fresh rosemary, chopped

2 teaspoon ground ginger
1 teaspoon paprika
½ teaspoon sea salt, to taste
1 whole lemon, sliced

1. Select the BAKE function, and adjust the temperature at 345°F/175°C and set the time for 40 minutes. 2. Press the START/STOP button to activate the function, and allow the oven to preheat. 3. Prepare a large zip-lock bag, add the chicken thighs, avocado oil, lemon zest, chopped fresh rosemary, ground ginger, sea salt, and lemon juice, and then seal the bag. 4. Place in the refrigerator to marinate for at least 20 minutes and up to 12 hours. 5. In a large cast-iron skillet, coat inside the skillet with a single layer of oil and heat over high heat. 6. Once the oil is heated, sear the chicken skin-side down until crispy and golden brown, about 3 to 5 minutes. Flip and sear for 3 to 5 minutes. 7. Carefully transfer the chicken to the roasting pan, and repeat the cooking steps for the rest chicken. 8. In a skillet, add all the crispy chicken and its juices. Add the lemon slices to the chicken. 9. Cover the chicken with foil and then bake in the preheated oven on position 6 for 40 minutes. 10. When cooked, carefully remove and serve.
Per Serving: Calories 413; Fat 31.86g; Sodium 284mg; Carbs 1.95g; Fiber 0.3g; Sugar 0.4g; Protein 28.24g

Dijon Turkey Breast

Prep Time: 30 minutes | Cook Time: 2 hours | Serves: 6

1 whole bone-in turkey breast	2 teaspoons kosher salt
3 garlic cloves, finely chopped	½ teaspoon freshly ground black pepper
1 tablespoon fresh rosemary leaves, chopped	2 tablespoons extra-virgin olive oil
1 tablespoon fresh thyme leaves, chopped	2 teaspoons Dijon mustard
1 tablespoon fresh sage leaves, chopped	½ cup freshly squeezed orange juice
	2 tablespoons freshly squeezed lemon juice
	½ cup chicken broth
	1 orange, sliced

1. Select the ROAST function, and adjust the temperature at 325°F/165°C and set the time for 2 hours. 2. Press the START/STOP button to activate the function, and allow the oven to preheat. 3. Add the turkey breast to the roasting pan, skin-side up. 4. Add the rosemary, sage, thyme, salt, garlic, olive oil, mustard, and pepper and combine well to make a paste. 5. Lift the skin away from the breast. Then spread half of the paste on the meat. Rub the remaining paste all over the outside of the turkey. 6. Add lemon juice, chicken broth, and orange juice into the baking pan. Spread over the pan with orange slices. 7. Roast the food in the oven on position 6 until the chicken is cooked with its skin golden brown. 8. Transfer to a serving bowl and part-skim the fat on top of the juice.

Per Serving: Calories 393; Fat 7.16g; Sodium 1145mg; Carbs 6.63g; Fiber 1g; Sugar 4.13g; Protein 71.68g

Crispy Spiced Chicken

Prep Time: 3 hours 30 minutes | Cook Time: 20 minutes | Serves: 8

Brine

½ gallon buttermilk	3 tablespoons salt, to taste
4 cloves garlic, crushed	3 pounds fresh whole chicken, cut up
½ white onion, sliced	
½ cup hot sauce	

Seasoning blend

1 tablespoon granulated sugar	1 tablespoon garlic powder
1 tablespoon salt, as you like	1 tablespoon poultry seasoning
1 tablespoon black pepper	1 teaspoon smoked salt
1 tablespoon onion powder	½ tablespoon chili powder
1 tablespoon cayenne plus extra for flavoring	3 cups self-rising flour
1 tablespoon Cajun seasoning	
1 teaspoon celery salt	
1 tablespoon paprika	

Egg mixture

3 eggs	Peanut oil or shortening for frying
¼ cup water	Cajun seasoning for sprinkling
½ cup hot sauce, plus more as desired	
1 teaspoon garlic powder	

1. Select the AIRFRY function, and adjust the temperature at 400°F/200°C and set the time for 20 minutes. 2. Press the START/STOP button to activate the function, and allow the oven to preheat. 3. Prepare a large bowl and line a roasting bag over it. Add garlic, onion slices, buttermilk, salt, and ½ cup of hot sauce. 4. Tie the bag and soak in the chicken. Place in the refrigerator for up to 3 hours. 5. Drain the chicken and transfer the chicken onto the roasting pan. 6. Mix together the seasoning blend and taste to adjust as you like. 7. Then sprinkle evenly over the chicken with up to half the seasoning blend. Set it aside. 8. Combine the flour with the remaining spices and add to a large paper bag. 9. Add the chicken to the bag. Close tightly and shake until coated well. 10. Take the chicken out from the bag and shake off any excess flour. 11. Add water, hot sauce, garlic powder, and the beaten eggs to a large bowl and mix well. 12. Dip the chicken pieces with the egg mixture and get rid of any excess mixture.13. In the bag again, add the chicken and shake to coat well. 14. Then return the coated chicken to the pan; insert the pan inside the oven on position 3 and cook the food.15. Serve on a serving plate and sprinkle over with Cajun seasoning immediately.

Per Serving: Calories 443; Fat 9.21g; Sodium 5369mg; Carbs 43.2g; Fiber 2.7g; Sugar 3.47g; Protein 44.01g

Popcorn Chicken

Prep Time: 30 minutes | Cook Time: 6 minutes | Serves: 4

1½ pounds boneless, skinless chicken	thighs
Marinade	
1 medium head of garlic	cornstarch
½-inch ginger, peeled and minced	½ teaspoon five-spice
3 green onions, minced	½ teaspoon ground white
2 tablespoons soy sauce	pepper
1 tablespoon mirin	¼ teaspoon ground Sichuan
1 teaspoon sweet potato starch or	peppercorns
Coating	
1 medium egg	cornstarch
½ cup cold water	Salt, white pepper, and five-spice, to
2-3 cups sweet potato starch or	taste

1. Select the AIRFRY function, and adjust the temperature at 335°F/170°C and set the time for 6 minutes. 2. Press the START/STOP button to activate the function, and allow the oven to preheat. 3. Cut the chicken into 1-inch chunks. 4. In a large bowl, add the chicken chunks. 5. Press the garlic to mince. 6. In a small bowl, add the minced garlic, ginger, minced green onions, sweet potato starch, mirin, white pepper, five-spice, and pepper, and mix well to make the marinade. 7. Then sprinkle onto the chicken chunks and mix together to coat. Place the chicken in the refrigerator for at least half an hour or overnight. 8. In a medium-sized bowl, beat the eggs with ½ cup of water with a fork. 9. Add the sweet potato starch to a separate medium bowl. 10. Dip the chicken in the egg mixture with tongs or chopsticks, and then in the starch. 11. Place the chicken in the air fryer basket and insert the basket inside the oven on position 3. 12. Air fry the chicken for 3 to 4 minutes until golden brown. Repeat with the remaining chicken pieces. 13. Once the chicken pieces are cooked, transfer to a serving bowl and sprinkle with enough salt, pepper, and a little bit five-spice. 14. Serve and enjoy!
Per Serving: Calories 359; Fat 12.42g; Sodium 595mg; Carbs 42.96g; Fiber 4.5g; Sugar 11.43g; Protein 18.89g

Spicy Chicken Wings

Prep Time: 4 hours 10 minutes | Cook Time: 40 minutes | Serves: 4

2 ¼–2 ½ pounds chicken wings, separated at the joints and wing tips discarded	fish sauce
	2 tablespoons canola or grapeseed oil
	1 large shallot, minced
¾ teaspoon kosher salt	2 Thai chilis, minced (with seeds)
2 teaspoons sugar	2 stalks of lemongrass, inner bulb
1 tablespoon Madras curry powder	chopped finely
	1 teaspoon garlic, minced
1 tablespoon Vietnamese	2 tablespoons fresh cilantro, chopped, for garnish

1. Select the AIRFRY function, and adjust the temperature at 400°F/200°C and set the time for 40 minutes. 2. Press the START/STOP button to activate the function, and allow the oven to preheat. 3. Combine chicken wings, salt, sugar, curry powder, fish sauce, oil, shallot, Thai chilis, lemongrass, and garlic in a large re-sealable plastic bag. 4. Seal the bag and distribute the spices evenly around the chicken. Then place in the refrigerator and marinate for at least 4 hours or overnight. 5. Allow the chicken to sit at room temperature. 6. On the air fryer basket, add the marinated chicken and insert it inside the oven on position 3. 7. Air fry the chicken in the oven for 40 minutes, flipping the chicken every 10 minutes to ensure the chicken is evenly cooked. 8. When cooked, the internal temperature should be 165°F/74°C. 9. Set the chicken aside to cool. 10. Serve warm, and enjoy!
Per Serving: Calories 425; Fat 17.03g; Sodium 1128mg; Carbs 7.93g; Fiber 2.3g; Sugar 1.93g; Protein 58.86g

Chicken with Pepper Jelly

Prep Time: 20 minutes | Cook Time: 35 minutes | Serves: 6

1 qt. buttermilk
¼ cup hot sauce
3 tablespoon garlic, minced
2 teaspoons celery salt
2⅓ teaspoons salt, divided
2⅓ teaspoons black pepper, divided
Pepper jelly drizzle
½ cup seeded red bell pepper, minced
1 tablespoon crushed red pepper
¾ cup cider vinegar
3¼ cups sugar
2 jalapeño peppers, thinly sliced

1 (4-pound) chicken, cut
into 8 pieces
4 eggs
½ cup milk
4 cup flour

2 Fresno chilies, thinly
sliced
1 clove of garlic, minced
1 pinch salt

1. Select the AIRFRY function, and adjust the temperature at 400°F/200°C and set the time for 35 minutes. 2. Press the START/STOP button to activate the function, and allow the oven to preheat. 3. Mix the spicy sauce, celery salt, 2 teaspoons of salt, 1 teaspoon of black pepper, and the buttermilk in a large mixing bowl. 4. Add the chicken to the mixture and toss to coat well. Place the chicken together with the mixture in the refrigerator and marinate overnight. 5. Then remove the chicken from the refrigerator and set it aside to room temperature, about 1 hour. Drain the chicken from excess marinade. 6. Beat eggs and pour milk into a shallow bowl. In a separate dish, add flour and the remaining salt and pepper and combine well. In a third bowl, 7. Dip the chicken pieces in the flour. Coat well and then shake off any excess flour. Then soak in the egg mixture and dip again in the flour. 8. Grease the air fryer basket with cooking spray. 9. Arrange the coated chicken pieces evenly onto the basket, and insert the basket inside the oven on position 3. 10. Cook in your oven for 35 minutes or until the internal temperature of the meat is 165°F/74°C. 11. Add crushed red pepper, bell peppers, and vinegar to a food processor or blender and pulse several times. 12. In a medium heavy saucepan, add the rest Pepper Jelly Drizzle and combine well. 13. Heat the saucepan over high heat on the stovetop and stir them often to boil vigorously. 14. Then remove and let it sit to cool to room temperature. Serve or store the pepper jelly drizzle in an airtight container in your refrigerator for up to 6 months. 15. Drizzle the pepper jelly over the chicken and serve!
Per Serving: Calories 851; Fat 15.09g; Sodium 1723mg; Carbs 126.17g; Fiber 9.6g; Sugar 63.99g; Protein 55.9g

Chicken Pot Pie

Prep Time: 10 minutes | Cook Time: 50 minutes | Serves: 8

6 tablespoons butter
1½ cups button
mushrooms, chopped
1½ cups onions, chopped
1½ cups carrots, chopped
¾ cup celery, chopped
1 tablespoon garlic,
chopped
1 teaspoon kosher salt
1 teaspoon freshly ground

black pepper
6 tablespoons flour, plus more for
dusting
2 pounds boneless and skinless chicken
thigh, cut into bite-size pieces
3 cups chicken broth
½ cup frozen green peas
4 ½ teaspoons parsley, chopped
1 sheet puff pastry, thawed
1 egg, whisked

1. Select the AIRFRY function, and adjust the temperature at 400°F/200°C and set the time for 20 minutes. 2. Press the START/STOP button to activate the function, and allow the oven to preheat. 3. Melt the butter in a saucepan over medium heat. 4. Sauté the onions, celery, carrots, garlic, and mushrooms for 3 minutes. 5. Add the black pepper, salt, and 6 tablespoons of flour to cook together, stirring often. 6. Then add the chicken and cook for about 5 minutes. 7. Pour broth and cook for about 20 minutes, stirring constantly. 8. Turn off the heat. Add parsley and peas and stir well. 9. On a work surface, dust the flour and make the puff pastry over. 10. Invert a suitable casserole dish over the puff pastry and cut around the dish 1 inch wider than the dish. 11. Pour the veggie mixture into the casserole dish. Cut a small hole in the center of the pie to vent. 12. Add the egg and 1 tablespoon of water together in a separate dish and whisk together to form an egg wash. Pour the egg wash over the puff pastry. 13. Arrange the casserole dish on the roasting pan, and then insert the pan with the dish inside the oven on position 3. 14. Cook the food until it is golden brown and use a fork to fluff. 15. When cooked, remove from the oven carefully. 16. Serve and enjoy!
Per Serving: Calories 320; Fat 15.51g; Sodium 817mg; Carbs 14.25g; Fiber 2g; Sugar 3.36g; Protein 29.96g

Roasted Chicken Thighs

Prep Time: 35 minutes | Cook Time: 15 minutes | Serves: 4

2 tablespoons sesame oil

2 tablespoons soy sauce

1 tablespoon honey

1 tablespoon sriracha sauce

1 teaspoon rice vinegar

2 pounds of chicken thighs

1 green onion, chopped

2 tablespoons toasted sesame seeds

1. Select the ROAST function, and adjust the temperature at 350°F/175°C and set the time for 15 minutes. 2. Press the START/STOP button to activate the function, and allow the oven to preheat. 3. Mix the soy sauce, sriracha, vinegar, honey, and sesame oil in a bowl. 4. Transfer the mixture into an airtight container and place it in the refrigerator for at least 30 minutes. 5. Place the chicken in the roasting pan and insert them together inside the oven in position 6 to cook. 6. When cooked, carefully remove the chicken from the oven and transfer it to a plate. Set it aside to cool for 5 minutes. 7. Add sesame seeds and chopped green onion to garnish. 8. Serve and enjoy!

Per Serving: Calories 629; Fat 47.92g; Sodium 362mg; Carbs 9.25g; Fiber 1.2g; Sugar 6.74g; Protein 38.97g

Teriyaki Chicken Wings

Prep Time: 10 minutes | Cook Time: 25 minutes | Serves: 4

2 pounds of chicken wings

½ cup Teriyaki sauce

2 teaspoons minced garlic

¼ teaspoon ground ginger

2 teaspoons baking powder

1. Select the AIRFRY function, and adjust the temperature at 400°F/200°C and set the time for 25 minutes. 2. Press the START/STOP button to activate the function, and allow the oven to preheat. 3. In a bowl, add the chicken wings, Teriyaki sauce, minced garlic, and ground ginger and combine well. Let the chicken wings marinate in the refrigerator for an hour. 4. Then arrange the chicken wings onto the air fryer basket and rub the chicken wings with baking powder. 5. Insert the basket inside the oven on Position 3. 6. Cook the wings and flipping them several times while cooking. 7. Serve and enjoy!

Per Serving: Calories 323; Fat 8.06g; Sodium 826mg; Carbs 7.33g; Fiber 0.1g; Sugar 5.09g; Protein 52.07g

Chicken Breasts with Peppers and Onions

Prep Time: 10 minutes | Cook Time: 15 minutes | Serves: 4

½ pound boneless and skinless chicken breasts

1 large bell pepper, cut into strips

1 medium red onion, cut into strips

1 tablespoon Mazola corn oil

1 tablespoon chili powder

2 teaspoons lime juice

1 teaspoon cumin

Salt and pepper to taste

1. Select the AIRFRY function, and adjust the temperature at 370°F/190°C and set the time for 15 minutes. 2. Press the START/STOP button to activate the function, and allow the oven to preheat. 3. Add bell pepper, chicken stripes, chili powder, cumin, pepper, onion, Mazola corn oil, and salt in a bowl and whisk well. 4. Place the fajitas on the roasting pan, insert the pan inside the preheated oven on position 3, and then cook them for 10 to 13 minutes. 5. Toss the food halfway through cooking to cook evenly. 6. Serve and enjoy!

Per Serving: Calories 127; Fat 5.46g; Sodium 86mg; Carbs 6.14g; Fiber 1.6g; Sugar 2.51g; Protein 13.88g

Delicious Fried Chicken Wings

Prep Time: 10 minutes | Cook Time: 18 minutes | Serves: 4

2 pounds of chicken wings
Marinade:
1 cup buttermilk
½ teaspoon salt
Coating:
1 cup flour
1 cup panko bread crumbs
2 tablespoons poultry seasoning

Cooking spray

½ teaspoon black pepper

2 teaspoons salt

1. Select the AIRFRY function, and adjust the temperature at 360°F/180°C and set the time for 18 minutes. 2. Press the START/STOP button to activate the function, and allow the oven to preheat. 3. Add salt, buttermilk, and black pepper, and whisk well to marinate the chicken. 4. Then add the chicken wings to the marinade bowl and toss to coat well. Set it aside to marinate for at least 1 hour. 5. Prepare the air fryer basket and spritz with cooking spray. 6. In a shallow bowl, add the flour, panko bread crumbs, poultry seasoning, and salt together and combine well. 7. Transfer the marinated chicken to toss in the bread crumb mixture and coat well. 8. Place the chicken in the basket and insert the basket inside the oven on position 3. 9. Cook the chicken and flip once after 10 minutes of cooking time. 10. When cooked, remove from the oven and transfer to a serving plate. 11. Serve and enjoy!
Per Serving: Calories 538; Fat 10.48g; Sodium 1952mg; Carbs 47.9g; Fiber 2.4g; Sugar 4.73g; Protein 58.94g

Herbed Turkey Breast

Prep Time: 20 minutes | Cook Time: 90 minutes | Serves: 4

3 strips of thick-cut bacon
3 tablespoons softened unsalted butter, at room temperature
1½ tablespoons minced garlic
1 tablespoon sage leaves, freshly chopped
1½ teaspoons rosemary leaves, freshly chopped

1 teaspoon oregano leaves, freshly chopped
1 teaspoon thyme leaves, freshly chopped
2 teaspoons kosher salt, divided
1 teaspoon freshly ground black pepper, divided
1 (6-pound) whole turkey breast, rinsed and patted dry

1. Select the BAKE function, and adjust the temperature at 375°F/190°C and set the time for 1 hour and 15 minutes. 2. Press the START/STOP button to activate the function, and allow the oven to preheat. 3. Line the roasting pan with aluminum foil. 4. In a skillet, cook the bacon to crisp. Then drain with paper towels. Reserve the rendered bacon fat, about 1 tablespoon. 5. Finely chop the cooked bacon and transfer it to a small bowl. 6. Add in sage, oregano, thyme, butter, 1 teaspoon of salt, ½ teaspoon of pepper, and garlic, and mix well with a spoon until a paste has been formed. 7. Loosen the skin on both sides of the turkey breast to separate it from the meat. 8. Separate the herb paste into 2 and spread gently on the turkey breast. 9. And evenly spread the rest half between the skin and breast. 10. Add the rest salt and pepper to the outside of the turkey to season. 11. Then brush the bacon fat over the turkey. 12. Arrange the seasoned turkey breast in the pan, and cook for about 1 hour to 1 hour and 10 or 15 minutes, or until the meat thermometer reads the center of the thickest part at 165°F/74°C. 13. When cooked, remove the turkey from the oven and let it sit for 20 minutes to cool. 14. Cut into your desired-size slices and serve! Enjoy!
Per Serving: Calories 592; Fat 14.37g; Sodium 1572mg; Carbs 2.24g; Fiber 0.7g; Sugar 0.05g; Protein 107.54g

Crispy Chicken Strips

Prep Time: 10 minutes | Cook Time: 10 minutes | Serves: 6

½ cup all-purpose flour
2 cups panko bread crumbs
2 tablespoons canola oil
1 egg
3 chicken breasts, each cut

into four strips, boneless and skinless
Kosher salt and ground black pepper, to taste
Cooking spray

1. Select the AIRFRY function, and adjust the temperature at 360°F/180°C and set the time for 10 minutes. 2. Press the START/STOP button to activate the function, and allow the oven to preheat. 3. Prepare the air fryer basket and spritz with cooking spray. 4. In a large bowl, add the flour. 5. In a shallow dish, add the canola oil and panko and mix well to combine. 6. In a separate bowl, whisk the egg. 7. Sprinkle salt and pepper over the chicken strips to season. Then dredge in the flour. Shake off any excess. 8. Drop in the egg mixture and coat with the breadcrumbs. 9. Transfer the strips onto the air fryer basket; insert the basket on position 3. 10. Cook until the strips are crunchy and lightly browned, flipping the chicken strips halfway through cooking. 11. Serve and enjoy!
Per Serving: Calories 384; Fat 20.19g; Sodium 166mg; Carbs 14.59g; Fiber 0.7g; Sugar 1.18g; Protein 33.99g

Chicken Parmigiana

Prep Time: 10 minutes | Cook Time: 55 minutes | Serves: 4

½ cup seasoned bread crumbs
¼ cup grated parmesan cheese
3 tablespoons spaghetti sauce mix
1-½ teaspoons garlic powder
4 boneless skinless chicken breast halves

½ cup Italian salad dressing
½ cup meatless spaghetti sauce
¼ cup shredded part-skim mozzarella cheese

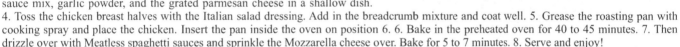

1. Select the BAKE function, and adjust the temperature at 350°F/175°C and set the time for 50 minutes. 2. Press the START/STOP button to activate the function, and allow the oven to preheat. 3. Combine the bread crumbs, spaghetti sauce mix, garlic powder, and the grated parmesan cheese in a shallow dish. 4. Toss the chicken breast halves with the Italian salad dressing. Add in the breadcrumb mixture and coat well. 5. Grease the roasting pan with cooking spray and place the chicken. Insert the pan inside the oven on position 6. 6. Bake in the preheated oven for 40 to 45 minutes. 7. Then drizzle over with Meatless spaghetti sauces and sprinkle the Mozzarella cheese over. Bake for 5 to 7 minutes. 8. Serve and enjoy!
Per Serving: Calories 493; Fat 28.84g; Sodium 566mg; Carbs 18.36g; Fiber 1.2g; Sugar 2.04g; Protein 37.48g

Turkey Thighs

Prep Time: 1 hour 10 minutes | Cook Time: 35 minutes | Serves: 4

1 cup buttermilk
½ cup maple syrup
1 egg
1 teaspoon granulated garlic
4 skin-on, bone-in turkey thighs
Dry mix:
½ cup all-purpose flour

¼ cup tapioca flour
1 tablespoon salt
1 teaspoon sweet paprika
½ teaspoon smoked paprika
1 teaspoon granulated onion
¼ teaspoon ground black pepper
¼ teaspoon cayenne pepper
½ teaspoon granulated garlic
½ teaspoon honey powder

1. Select the AIRFRY function, and adjust the temperature at 400°F/200°C and set the time for 35 minutes. 2. Press the START/STOP button to activate the function, and allow the oven to preheat. 3. Combine the maple syrup, buttermilk, 1 teaspoon granulated garlic, and egg in a re-sealable bag. Then add the chicken thighs and seal. Put the sealed bag in the refrigerator and let it marinate for at least 1 hour or up to overnight. 4. Add tapioca flour, sweet paprika, flour, granulated onion, pepper, cayenne pepper, honey powder, ½ teaspoon granulated garlic, salt, smoked paprika, and salt in a shallow dish. 5. Remove the marinated chicken from the bag and drain excess sauce. Add the chicken to the flour mixture and coat well. Shake off any excess. 6. Prepare the air fryer basket and spray with cooking spray. 7. Place the meat in the basket and insert the basket inside the oven on position 3 8. Cook them for 35 minutes, or until the internal temperature of the meat reaches 165°F/74°C. 9. When cooked, remove from the oven carefully. Serve and enjoy!
Per Serving: Calories 711; Fat 35.4g; Sodium 2055mg; Carbs 58.54g; Fiber 1.7g; Sugar 32.39g; Protein 38.73g

Herbed Turkey Breast and Bacon

Prep Time: 10 minutes | Cook Time: 40 minutes | Serves: 4

3 strips of thick-cut bacon
1½ tablespoons garlic, minced
1 tablespoon fresh sage, chopped
1½ teaspoons fresh rosemary, chopped
1 teaspoon fresh oregano, chopped
1 teaspoon fresh thyme, chopped
3 tablespoons unsalted butter, softened

2 teaspoons kosher salt, divided
1 teaspoon freshly ground black pepper, divided
1 (2 ½–3-pound) half-turkey breast, rinsed & patted dry

1. Select the BAKE function, and adjust the temperature at 325°F/165°C and set the time for 30 minutes. 2. Press the START/STOP button to activate the function, and allow the oven to preheat. 3. Add the bacon to a skillet and cook over medium-high heat until crisp. Reserve 1 tablespoon of bacon fat and then drain the bacon with a paper towel. 4. Then finely cut the bacon and transfer it to a small bowl. 5. Mix in the sage, oregano, butter, thyme, 1 teaspoon salt, rosemary, garlic, and ½ teaspoon black pepper and stir to make a paste. 6. Separate the skin from the flesh by loosening the skin gently on the turkey breast with fingertips. 7. Rub the remaining salt and black pepper over the outside of the chicken breast to season and brush over with the reserved bacon fat. 8. Arrange the seasoned chicken breast on the roasting pan and insert it into the oven in position 6. 9. Cook for 30 minutes or more, or until the internal temperature reads 165°F/74°C. 10. When cooked, remove the turkey from the oven carefully. Set it aside to cool for about 20 minutes. 11. Cut the turkey into thin slices. 12. Serve with your favored dipping. Enjoy!
Per Serving: Calories 216; Fat 13.43g; Sodium 1276mg; Carbs 2.24g; Fiber 0.7g; Sugar 0.05g; Protein 21.08g

Fried Chicken with Peanut Butter

Prep Time: 15 minutes | Cook Time: 22 minutes | Serves: 4

1-pound bone-in skin-on chicken thighs
¼ cup creamy peanut butter
1 tablespoon sriracha sauce
1 tablespoon soy sauce

2 tablespoons Thai sweet chili sauce
2 tablespoons lime juice
1 teaspoon minced garlic
1 teaspoon minced ginger
½ teaspoon kosher salt
½ cup hot water

1. Select the AIRFRY function, and adjust the temperature at 350°F/175°C and set the time for 22 minutes. 2. Press the START/STOP button to activate the function, and allow the oven to preheat. 3. Add lime juice, soy sauce, sriracha, salt, sweet chili sauce, and peanut butter to a large bowl and mix well. 4. Stir in hot water until well mixed. 5. In a zip-top bag, add half the sauce and chicken. Shake to mix evenly, and then place in the refrigerator to marinate. 6. Remove from the refrigerator and take the chicken out from the bag. 7. Arrange the chicken onto the air fryer basket, and insert the basket in the oven on position 3 to cook better. 8. When cooked, remove from the oven carefully. 9. Serve and enjoy!
Per Serving: Calories 373; Fat 28.27g; Sodium 646mg; Carbs 6.94g; Fiber 1.7g; Sugar 2.49g; Protein 23.3g

Chicken Breasts

Prep Time: 10 minutes | Cook Time: 10 minutes | Serves: 4

4 (4-ounce) boneless, skinless chicken breasts
Chicken seasoning or rub to taste
Salt and ground black pepper to taste
¼ cup honey

2 tablespoons soy sauce
2 teaspoons grated fresh ginger
2 garlic cloves, minced
Cooking spray

1. Select the AIRFRY function, and adjust the temperature at 400°F/200°C and set the time for 10 minutes. 2. Press the START/STOP button to activate the function, and allow the oven to preheat. 3. Prepare the air fryer basket and spritz with cooking spray. 4. Sprinkle chicken seasoning, salt, and chicken breast. 5. Transfer the seasoned chicken onto the prepared basket and spritz the chicken with cooking spray. Insert the basket inside the oven on position 3.6. Cook the food and flip once halfway through cooking. 7. When cooked, the meat thermometer should read around 165°F/74ºC. 8. Heat the soy sauce, ginger, garlic, and honey in a large saucepan over medium-high heat for 3 minutes until thickened. Stir often. 9. When cooked, carefully remove the chicken from the oven and serve with the honey mixture.
Per Serving: Calories 137; Fat 2.56g; Sodium 221mg; Carbs 21.26g; Fiber 0.4g; Sugar 19.56g; Protein 8.94g

Chapter 6 Beef, Pork, and Lamb Recipes

Tasty Spaghetti Squash

Prep Time: 15 minutes | Cook Time: 35 minutes | Serves: 4

1 pound of ground beef
1 medium yellow onion, chopped
1 tablespoon garlic, minced
1 can (15 ounces) tomato sauce
1 can (6 ounces) tomato paste
1 can (14.5 ounces) diced tomatoes,
Italian-style and un-drained
¼ to ½ teaspoon crushed
red pepper
1 medium spaghetti squash,
cut in half lengthwise,
seeds removed

Toppings
Fresh basil, thinly sliced
Parmesan cheese, grated

1. Select the BAKE function, and adjust the temperature at 400°F/200°C and set the time for 20 minutes. 2. Press the START/STOP button to activate the function, and allow the oven to preheat. 3. Remove seeds from the spaghetti squash. Then cut it in half lengthwise. 4. Preheat a stockpot over medium heat.
5. Add garlic, onion, and ground beef to the stockpot. Cook and stir for 8 to 10 minutes, breaking the beef into ¾-inch crumbles.
6. Add diced tomatoes, tomato paste, crushed red pepper, and tomato sauce to the pot and stir well to season. Cook until half-done.
7. Transfer the sauce mixture to the roasting pan and insert it into the oven on position 6. 8. Cook, and halfway through cooking, stir in basil, as you desire. 9. Add the spaghetti squash, slightly overlapping the halves in an 8-by-8-inch microwave-safe baking dish. 10. Microwave the squash on high for 10 to 12 minutes until the squash is just tender. Allow it to stand for 5 minutes. Then, separate the strands with a fork. 11. Add the cooked Bolognese sauce over the squash. 12. Serve and enjoy!
Per Serving: Calories 321; Fat 13.47g; Sodium 217mg; Carbs 16.79g; Fiber 4.8g; Sugar 10.18g; Protein 34.05g

Pork Tenderloin with Peach Salsa

Prep Time: 15 minutes | Cook Time: 22 minutes | Serves: 4

¾ cup fresh peaches,
peeled and chopped
1 small sweet red pepper,
chopped
1 jalapeno pepper, seeded
and chopped
2 tablespoons red onion,
finely chopped
2 tablespoons fresh
cilantro, minced
1 tablespoon lime juice
1 garlic clove, minced
⅛ teaspoon salt
⅛ teaspoon pepper
2 tablespoons olive oil
1 tablespoon brown sugar
1 tablespoon Caribbean jerk seasoning
1 teaspoon dried thyme
1 teaspoon dried rosemary, crushed
½ teaspoon seasoned salt
1 pound pork tenderloin

1. Select the AIRFRY function, and adjust the temperature at 335°F/170°C and set the time for 22 minutes. 2. Press the START/STOP button to activate the function, and allow the oven to preheat. 3. Combine the chopped peaches, red pepper, jalapeno pepper, red onion, minced cilantro, lime juice, garlic, salt, and pepper in a small bowl. 4. Mix the brown sugar, thyme, rosemary, seasoned salt, oil, and jerk seasoning in a separate bowl. 5. Rub the pork tenderloin with the sugar mixture. 6. Place the coated pork tenderloin in the air fryer basket and insert the basket in the oven on position 3. 7. Cook and flip once halfway through cooking. 8. When the pork has been done, the internal meat thermometer should read 145°F/60°C. 9. Cool the dish for about 5 minutes. 10. Cut into your desired-sized slices. 11. Serve and enjoy with the peach salad!
Per Serving: Calories 285; Fat 10.88g; Sodium 592mg; Carbs 15.66g; Fiber 1.6g; Sugar 12.63g; Protein 30.39g

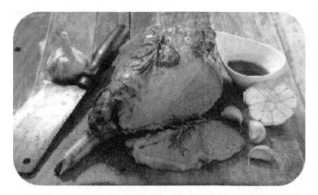

Simple Lamb Roast

Prep Time: 5 minutes | Cook Time: 15 minutes | Serves: 2

10 ounces lamb leg roast	or dried
1 tablespoon olive oil	1 teaspoon thyme, fresh or dried
1 teaspoon rosemary, fresh	½ teaspoon black pepper

1. Select the AIRFRY function, and adjust the temperature at 360°F/180°C and set the time for 15 minutes. 2. Press the START/STOP button to activate the function, and allow the oven to preheat. 3. Mix the thyme, rosemary, and olive oil in a plate. 4. Pat the lamb roast dry. Coat it with the herb-oil mixture. 5. Place the coated lamb onto the air fryer basket. 6. Insert the basket inside the preheated oven on position 3. 7. Air fry the lamb meat for 15 minutes. 8. When the cooking time is up, carefully remove it from the oven, cover it with kitchen foil, and let it stand to cool for about 5 minutes. 9. Discover. Serve and enjoy!

Per Serving: Calories 320; Fat 17.11g; Sodium 98mg; Carbs 0.65g; Fiber 0.3g; Sugar 0g; Protein 38.64g

Ribeye Steak

Prep Time: 5 minutes | Cook Time: 55 minutes | Serves: 8

1 (48 to 60 ounces) tomahawk steak	1 tablespoon butter if
Salt and freshly ground pepper	desired

1. Select the BAKE function, and adjust the temperature at 250°F/120°C and set the time for 50 minutes. 2. Press the START/STOP button to activate the function, and allow the oven to preheat. 3. Leave the steak on the countertop to room temperature. 4. Season the meat with the remaining ingredients, and then place the meat in the roasting pan. 5. Insert the pan inside the oven on position 6, and then bake the food for 50 minutes. 6. When the cooking time is up, let it stand for 5 to 15 minutes. 7. Then broil the dish at High for 2 minutes or until the steak is just browned, flipping the steak halfway through. 8. Carefully remove from the oven. 9. Serve and enjoy!

Per Serving: Calories 443; Fat 23.01g; Sodium 879mg; Carbs 0.18g; Fiber 0.1g; Sugar 0g; Protein 59.22g

Roasted Round Beef

Prep Time: 10 minutes | Cook Time: 20 minutes | Serves: 6

½ teaspoon fresh rosemary	1 teaspoon salt
1 teaspoon dried thyme	4-pound top round roast beef
¼ teaspoon black pepper	1 teaspoon olive oil

1. Select the ROAST function, and adjust the temperature at 360°F/180°C and set the time for 20 minutes. 2. Press the START/STOP button to activate the function, and allow the oven to preheat. 3. Combine the thyme, rosemary, salt, and pepper in a bowl. 4. Rub the beef on all sides with the olive oil and the thyme mixture. 5. Transfer the beef to the roasting pan, and then roast them 6.

When done, let the beef sit for 10 minutes before serving.

Per Serving: Calories 382; Fat 10.62g; Sodium 557mg; Carbs 0.12g; Fiber 0.1g; Sugar 0g; Protein 71.36g

Roasted Beef and Broccoli

Prep Time: 5 minutes | Cook Time: 15 minutes | Serves: 8

½ cup low-sodium soy sauce
4 to 5 cloves garlic, finely minced
2 to 3 tablespoons of honey
2 tablespoons packed brown sugar
2 tablespoons sesame oil
2 tablespoons rice vinegar
2 to 3 teaspoons of ground ginger
1 teaspoon kosher salt
1 teaspoon freshly ground black pepper, or to taste
1-pound flank steak, sliced against the grain in bite-size pieces

About 4 to 6 cups of broccoli florets
1 tablespoon cornstarch (optional)
1 tablespoon cold water (optional)
2 to 3 green onions, sliced in 1-inch segments on the bias (optional for garnishing)
1 tablespoon sesame seeds (optional for garnishing)

1. Select the ROAST function, and adjust the temperature at 425°F/220°C and set the time for 12 minutes. 2. Press the START/STOP button to activate the function, and allow the oven to preheat. 3. Line the roasting pan with aluminum foil. 4. In a large bowl, add garlic, soy sauce, honey, sesame oil, rice vinegar, salt, pepper, ginger, brown sugar, and any optional red pepper flakes or cayenne, and whisk well. 5. Add the steak and stir well. Marinate for 10 to 15 minutes. 6. Evenly arrange the marinated steak onto the roasting pan. Set aside for later use. 7. Dunk the broccoli in the marinade mixture. Transfer the broccoli to the pan with a slotted spoon. Place the broccoli between the steak. Reserve the marinade. 8. Insert the pan inside the oven on position 6. Roast the food in the oven until the broccoli is just tender and the steak is completely cooked about 12 minutes. 9. Carefully remove the pan from the oven and transfer to a serving plate. 10. Drizzle with the reserved sauce as you desire. 11. Serve and enjoy!
Per Serving: Calories 150; Fat 6.42g; Sodium 902mg; Carbs 8.823g; Fiber 0.8g; Sugar 6.47g; Protein 14.41g

Lamb Curry Puffs

Prep Time: 15 minutes | Cook Time: 25 minutes | Serves: 12

1 pack biscuit dough
1 egg
1 teaspoon butter
3 tablespoons olive oil
Filling
1 cup lamb mince
1 large onion, thinly chopped

½ cup peas-carrots mix
Spices
1 tablespoon curry powder
¼ teaspoon ginger powder
⅛ teaspoon garlic powder
2 tablespoons hot sauce
Salt, as per taste
Pepper, as per taste

1. Select the AIRFRY function, and adjust the temperature at 375°F/190°C and set the time for 12 minutes. 2. Press the START/STOP button to activate the function, and allow the oven to preheat.
To make the filling:
1. In a skillet, heat the oil and add the chopped onions. Sauté them until golden brown. 2. Add the lamb mince and sauté over medium-low heat for 2 to 3 minutes. Add the carrot-peas mix and sauté for another 3 to 4 minutes. 3. Add the spice ingredients and sauté them together for another 4 to 5 minutes, stirring every minute. Remove it from heat and leave the mixture to cool.
To make the lamb curry puffs:
1. Add the egg and butter to a small bowl and whisk well. 2. Divide the biscuit dough into half and roll it into a circular-shaped disc. 3. In the center, add 2 tablespoons of lamb filling. Fold and pinch the edges of the disc to seal. 4. Arrange the lamb curry puffs in the air fryer basket and brush evenly with egg and butter mixture. 5. Insert the basket inside the preheated oven on position 3.
6. Let it cook until golden brown.7. Carefully remove from the oven and transfer to a serving plate. 8. Serve and enjoy!
Per Serving: Calories 129; Fat 8.99g; Sodium 125mg; Carbs 4.98g; Fiber 1.1g; Sugar 1.3g; Protein 7.06g

Vegetable & Bacon Burgers

Prep Time: 10 minutes | Cook Time: 40 minutes | Serves: 4

4 slices of thick-cut bacon	Salt, for seasoning
8 ounces shiitake or cremini mushrooms, thinly sliced	Ground black pepper for seasoning
	4 (6-ounce) hamburger patties
1½ cups onions, thinly sliced	4 slices of Swiss cheese
	4 onion buns, halved and toasted
½ teaspoon garlic, minced	Mayonnaise, for serving (optional)
	Mustard, for serving (optional)

1. Select the AIRFRY function, and adjust the temperature at 400°F/200°C and set the time for 10 minutes. 2. Press the START/STOP button to activate the function, and allow the oven to preheat. 3. Place the bacon slices on the roasting pan, insert the pan inside the oven on position 3, and cook them for 10 minutes. 4. Line a plate with a paper towel. 5. When the bacon slices are cooked, place the bacon slices onto the paper towel-lined plate, removing half of the fat from the pan and reserving half of the fat on the pan. 6. Add the mushrooms to the air fryer basket and then insert the basket inside the oven on position 3 to air fryer them for 6 minutes. 7. Transfer the cooked mushrooms to a dish. 8. Place the hamburger patties on the air fryer basket and air-fry them for 2 minutes. 9. While cooking the hamburger patties, mix up the mushrooms, onions, garlic, salt, and black pepper in a bowl. 10. When the hamburger patties are cooked, place a mound of mushrooms, onions, and Swiss cheese on each hamburger patty. 11. Place the hamburger patties between the buns, top each patty with the bacon, and dress in the mayonnaise and mustard (optional). 12. Enjoy.
Per Serving: Calories 485; Fat 30.32g; Sodium 501mg; Carbs 33.53g; Fiber 4.7g; Sugar 9.83g; Protein 22.21g

Roasted Leg of Lamb

Prep Time: 10 minutes | Cook Time: 6 hours 30 minutes | Serves: 8

12 cloves of garlic, peeled	10 sprigs of thyme
7 pounds of leg of lamb	3 sprigs rosemary
Salt and pepper	3 teaspoons dried oregano
3 teaspoons paprika powder	3 dried bay leaves
3 teaspoons garlic powder	½ cup lemon juice
2 tablespoons olive oil	1½ cups white wine
2 large onions, quartered	2 cups chicken broth

1. Select the ROAST function, and adjust the temperature at 400°F/200°C and set the time for 30 minutes. 2. Press the START/STOP button to activate the function, and allow the oven to preheat. 3. Slit the lamb with a small knife on the top. 4. Cut about half the garlic cloves into slivers and stuff them into the slits. 5. Sprinkle salt, garlic powder, pepper, and paprika all over the lamb. Drizzle with olive oil and rub for a marinade. 6. Add the lamb to the roasting pan and insert it into the preheated oven on position 6. 7. Cook the meat until a nice brown crust has shown, about 30 minutes. 8. Carefully remove the pan from the oven. 9. Adjust the temperature to 350°F/175°C and time to 6 hours. 10. Turn the lamb upside down. Add all the remaining ingredients to the pan around the lamb. Pour in hot water until it comes up about a quarter to a third of the way up the height of the lamb. 11. Cover the lamb with parchment paper, then 2 layers of foil. 12. Let it roast in the oven for 3 hours and 30 minutes. 13. Add water to prevent it from drying out. Discover and turn the lamb. 14. Cover and roast for 2 hours and 30 minutes. 15. When the cooking time is up, remove the cover and roast for 20 to 30 minutes until brown. 16. Carefully remove from the oven. Transfer to a serving plate and use a foil to cover loosely. Let it rest for 30 to 40 minutes. 17. Reserve the liquid in a clear jug and skim the oil. Add lemon juice, salt, and pepper to season. 18. Serve and enjoy!
Per Serving: Calories 604; Fat 34.73g; Sodium 518mg; Carbs 9.17g; Fiber 1.6g; Sugar 3.3g; Protein 82.07g

Steak with Chimichurri Sauce

Prep Time: 2 hours 10 minutes | Cook Time: 20 minutes | Serves: 4

1 cup extra virgin olive oil
⅔ cup sherry wine vinegar
2 tablespoons lime juice
1 cup cilantro, chopped
¼ cup fresh basil leaves, chopped
1 tablespoon fresh marjoram leaves, chopped
3 tablespoons garlic, minced
2 tablespoons shallots, minced
¼ teaspoon crushed red pepper
2½ teaspoons kosher salt, divided
¾ teaspoon fresh cracked black pepper, divided
1 (1¾–2-pound) flank steak

1. Select the AIRFRY function, and adjust the temperature at 400°F/200°C and set the time for 18 minutes. 2. Press the START/STOP button to activate the function, and allow the oven to preheat. 3. Add olive oil, lime juice, basil, garlic, shallots, sherry vinegar, cilantro, and marjoram in a food processor and pulse until it is just fully combined. 4. Add ½ teaspoon salt, ¼ teaspoon black pepper, and crushed red pepper to a mixing bowl and mix to make the chimichurri sauce. 5. Reserve 1 cup of the chimichurri sauce in a non-reactive bowl. Cover with plastic wrap and let it stand for up to 6 hours at room temperature or in the refrigerator overnight. 6. Add 1 teaspoon salt and ¼ teaspoon black pepper to season the steak. Add the steak to a large resealable plastic bag. 7. Add the remaining chimichurri sauce to the bag. Seal the bag and place it in the refrigerator for at least 2 hours. 8. Then brush off the excess sauce from the steak and place it on the air fryer basket. Insert the basket inside the oven on position 3. 9. Cook until it reaches your desired doneness. 10. Transfer to a clean cutting board. Allow it to rest for 5 to 7 minutes. 11. Slice across the grain into thin strips. 12. Serve and enjoy!
Per Serving: Calories 296; Fat 25.47g; Sodium 1946mg; Carbs 4.73g; Fiber 0.8g; Sugar 0.81g; Protein 10.24g

Homemade Korean Bulgogi

Prep Time: 4 hours 10 minutes | Cook Time: 10 minutes | Serves: 4

¼ cup low-sodium soy sauce
2 tablespoons fresh orange juice
1 tablespoon dark brown sugar
1 tablespoon red pepper flakes
1 tablespoon garlic, minced
1 tablespoon ginger, minced
White parts of 1 bunch scallions, minced
2 teaspoons hot sesame oil
1-pound sirloin steak, cut into thin strips about 2-inches long and 1-inch wide
2 tablespoons toasted sesame seeds

1. Select the AIRFRY function, and adjust the temperature at 400°F/200°C and set the time for 10 minutes. 2. Press the START/STOP button to activate the function, and allow the oven to preheat. 3. Add orange sauce, soy sauce, red pepper flakes, white sections of the scallions, garlic, ginger, and brown sugar in a medium-sized mixing bowl. 4. Add the steak and stir to coat. 5. Let the steak strips marinate in the refrigerator for at least 4 hours or up to overnight. 6. Transfer the steak strips onto the roasting pan, and insert the pan inside the oven in position 3 to cook. 7. When the cooking time is up, carefully remove it from the oven and transfer it to a serving plate. 8. Sprinkle sesame seeds on top. 9. Serve and enjoy!
Per Serving: Calories 189; Fat 7.2g; Sodium 690mg; Carbs 4.95g; Fiber 1g; Sugar 1.7g; Protein 25.34g

Mongolian Beef

Prep Time: 10 minutes | Cook Time: 10 minutes | Serves: 4

1 pound flank steak, sliced
¼ cup cornstarch
2 tablespoons olive oil
4 cloves minced garlic
1 tablespoon minced ginger
½ cup low sodium soy sauce
½ cup water
½ cup brown sugar
2 green onions, chopped

1. Select the AIRFRY function, and adjust the temperature at 400°F/200°C and set the time for 10 minutes. 2. Press the START/STOP button to activate the function, and allow the oven to preheat. 3. Coat the beef slices with the cornstarch and then set aside for 5 minutes. 4. Spritz the beef slices with oil and then arrange them in the roasting pan, and insert the pan inside the oven on position 3. 5. Flip the meat slices every few minutes and spritz them with additional oil halfway through the cooking process. 6. Heat the olive oil and stir fry the ginger and garlic in the skillet. 7. Add the meat slices and cook for 2 minutes. 8. In the saucepan, stir together the soy sauce, water, and brown sugar; bring them to boil and simmer for 6 to 7 minutes, stirring periodically, or until the sauce has thickened. 9. Carefully add the cooked beef mixture to the sauce and continue cooking for 1 to 2 minutes, tossing the beef in the sauce. 10. Sprinkle chopped green onions and sesame seeds (optional) over the top before serving.
Per Serving: Calories 383; Fat 12.71g; Sodium 1222mg; Carbs 39.35g; Fiber 1g; Sugar 28.28g; Protein 27.8g

Sirloin Steaks

Prep Time: 10 minutes | Cook Time: 45 minutes | Serves: 4

2 top sirloin steaks
3 tablespoons butter, melted
3 tablespoons olive oil
Salt and pepper to taste

1. Select the ROAST function, and adjust the temperature at 350°F/175°C and set the time for 45 minutes. 2. Press the START/STOP button to activate the function, and allow the oven to preheat. 3. Season the sirloin steaks with olive oil, salt, and pepper; arrange the seasoned steaks on the roasting pan. 4. Insert the pan inside the oven on position 6 and cook the steaks. 5. When done, serve the steaks with melted butter.
Per Serving: Calories 732; Fat 51.84g; Sodium 227mg; Carbs 1.07g; Fiber 0.2g; Sugar 0.58g; Protein 61.74g

Mini Beef Burger

Prep Time: 20 minutes | Cook Time: 20 minutes | Serves: 12

1½ pounds lean ground beef
½ cup yellow onion, chopped
2 teaspoon garlic, minced
2 tablespoons ketchup
2 tablespoons sweet pickle relish
1 tablespoon yellow mustard
1 tablespoon Creole seasoning
½ teaspoon salt
¼ teaspoon ground black pepper, for seasoning
12 small dinner rolls, or hamburger buns
Slices of lettuce

1. Select the AIRFRY function, and adjust the temperature at 400°F/200°C and set the time for 20 minutes. 2. Press the START/STOP button to activate the function, and allow the oven to preheat. 3. Mix the onion, beef, garlic, pickle relish, ketchup, mustard, Creole seasoning, salt, and black pepper in a bowl. 4. Make the mixture into patties, about ¼ cup for each. Arrange the patties evenly on the air fryer basket. 5. Insert the basket inside the preheated oven on position 3. 6. Cook the patties for 18 to 20 minutes. 7. When the cooking has done, make your own bam burgers as you like. 8. Serve and enjoy!
Per Serving: Calories 213; Fat 8.25g; Sodium 391mg; Carbs 15.66g; Fiber 1.4g; Sugar 2.14g; Protein 17.77g

Cubed Steak

Prep Time: 10 minutes | Cook Time: 8 hours | Serves: 8

8 pieces of cubed steak
1¾ teaspoons adobo
seasoning or garlic salt
Black pepper, to taste
1 (8 ounces) can of tomato
sauce
1 cup water

1 small red bell pepper, sliced ¼-inch
thin strips
½ medium onion, sliced into ¼-inch thin
strips
⅓ cup green pitted olives + 2 tablespoons
of brine

1. Select the SLOW COOK function, and adjust the temperature at LO and set the time for 8 hours. 2. Press the START/STOP button to activate the function, and allow the oven to preheat. 3. Season the steak pieces with the adobo and black pepper. 4. Place the steak pieces in the roasting pan, top them with the onions and peppers, then pour the tomato sauce and water over them. 5. Insert the pan inside the oven on position 8 and cook them. 6. Add the olives along with some of the brine (liquid from the jar). 7. Once done, serve.
Per Serving: Calories 79; Fat 4.08g; Sodium 133mg; Carbs 4.73g; Fiber 0.8g; Sugar 1.05g; Protein 5.89g

Delicious Pork Chops

Prep Time: 5 minutes | Cook Time: 30 minutes | Serves: 3

1-pound boneless pork chops or 3 pieces,
½-inch thick
1 tablespoon olive oil
½ teaspoon salt
1 teaspoon paprika
1 teaspoon garlic powder

1 teaspoon onion powder
¼ teaspoon ground black
pepper
½ teaspoon Italian
seasoning

1. Select the BAKE function, and adjust the temperature at 325°F/165°C and set the time for 30 minutes. 2. Press the START/STOP button to activate the function, and allow the oven to preheat. 3. Mix up all the ingredients except for the oil and pork chops in a mixing bowl. 4. Coat the pork chops on both sides with the olive oil and then with the spice mixture. 5. Arrange the pork chops evenly in the roasting pan, and then insert the pan inside the oven on position 6 to cook. 6. When done, serve and enjoy.
Per Serving: Calories 243; Fat 9.79g; Sodium 497mg; Carbs 2.43g; Fiber 0.6g; Sugar 0.4g; Protein 34.34g

Pork Ribs with BBQ Sauce

Prep Time: 10 minutes | Cook Time: 15 minutes | Serves: 6

¼ cup honey, divided
¾ cup BBQ sauce
2 tablespoons tomato
ketchup
1 tablespoon

Worcestershire sauce
1 tablespoon soy sauce
½ teaspoon garlic powder
Freshly ground white pepper to taste
1¾ pound pork ribs

1. Select the ROAST function, and adjust the temperature at 355°F/180°C and set the time for 13 minutes. 2. Press the START/STOP button to activate the function, and allow the oven to preheat. 3. Mix up the BBQ sauce, tomato ketchup, Worcestershire sauce, soy sauce, garlic powder, white pepper, and 3 tablespoons of honey in the bowl. 4. Add the pork ribs and then place the bowl in the refrigerator to marinate the ribs for 20 minutes. 5. Place the ribs in the roasting pan and insert the pan inside the oven on position 6. 6. When cooked, remove the ribs from the oven and coat them with the remaining honey. 7. Serve hot.
Per Serving: Calories 253; Fat 8.04g; Sodium 389mg; Carbs 16.14g; Fiber 0.9g; Sugar 14.12g; Protein 28.44g

Honey Pork Tenderloin

Prep Time: 10 minutes | Cook Time: 15 minutes | Serves: 4

3 tablespoons Dijon mustard
3 tablespoons honey
1 teaspoon dried rosemary
1 tablespoon olive oil

1-pound pork tenderloin, rinsed and drained
Salt and black pepper to taste

1. Select the BAKE function, and adjust the temperature at 425°F/220°C and set the time for 15 minutes. 2. Press the START/STOP button to activate the function, and allow the oven to preheat. 3. In the bowl, mix up the honey, Dijon mustard, and rosemary. 4. Rub the pork tenderloin with salt and pepper on all sides. 5. In the skillet over high heat, heat the olive oil; add the pork tenderloin and cook for 3 minutes on each side, until golden brown. 6. Turn off the heat, evenly coat the pork tenderloin with the honey mixture and then transfer the pork tenderloin to the roasting pan. 7. Insert the pan inside the oven on position 6 and cook the food. 8. When done, the pork tenderloin should have an inner temperature of 140ºF/62°C. 9. Allow the pork tenderloin to sit for 3 minutes before slicing and serving.
Per Serving: Calories 249; Fat 7.77g; Sodium 194mg; Carbs 14.06g; Fiber 0.7g; Sugar 13.04g; Protein 30.23g

Roasted Skirt Steaks

Prep Time: 10 minutes | Cook Time: 10 minutes | Serves: 2

2 (8 ounces) Skirt Steaks
1 cup finely chopped parsley
¼ cup finely chopped mint
2 tablespoons fresh oregano (Washed & finely chopped)
3 finely chopped cloves of garlic

1 teaspoon red pepper flakes (Crushed)
1 tablespoon ground cumin
1 teaspoon cayenne pepper
2 teaspoons smoked paprika
1 teaspoon salt
¼ teaspoon pepper
¾ cup oil
3 tablespoons red wine vinegar

1. Select the ROAST function, and adjust the temperature at 390°F/200°C and set the time for 10 minutes. 2. Press the START/STOP button to activate the function, and allow the oven to preheat. 3. Mix up all the ingredients except for the steaks in the bowl. 4. Add ¼ cup of the mixture in a plastic baggie with the steak and place in the refrigerator overnight. 5. Allow it to sit for at least 30 minutes at room temperature, and then arrange the steaks on the roasting pan. 6. Insert the pan inside the oven on position 6 and cook the food. 7. Once done, serve and enjoy.
Per Serving: Calories 800; Fat 69.64g; Sodium 1663mg; Carbs 8.05g; Fiber 3.3g; Sugar 0.84g; Protein 38.95g

Beef Kebabs

Prep Time: 10 minutes | Cook Time: 18 minutes | Serves: 4

2 teaspoons ground cumin
2 teaspoons ground coriander
¼ teaspoon ground cinnamon
⅛ teaspoon ground smoked paprika
2 teaspoons lime zest
½ teaspoon salt

½ teaspoon black pepper
1 tablespoon lemon juice
2 teaspoons olive oil
1.5 pounds of lean beef, cubed

1. Select the AIRFRY function, and adjust the temperature at 370°F/185°C and set the time for 18 minutes. 2. Press the START/STOP button to activate the function, and allow the oven to preheat. 3. Prepare all the ingredients and then mix them together in a large mixing bowl. 4. Thread the beef on the skewers. 5. Place the beef skewers in the air fryer basket, and insert the basket inside the oven on position 3 to cook. 6. Flip the skewers when cooked halfway through. 7. Serve warm.
Per Serving: Calories 253; Fat 12.23g; Sodium 439mg; Carbs 1.37g; Fiber 0.4g; Sugar 0.18g; Protein 35.18g

Herbed Rib-eye Steak

Prep Time: 25 minutes | Cook Time: 20 minutes | Serves: 2

4 tablespoons butter, softened	chives
2 cloves garlic, minced	1 teaspoon freshly chopped thyme
2 teaspoons freshly chopped parsley	1 teaspoon freshly chopped rosemary
1 teaspoon freshly chopped	1 (2 pounds) bone-in ribeye steak
	Kosher salt
	Freshly ground black pepper

1. Select the ROAST function, and adjust the temperature at 400°F/200°C and set the time for 20 minutes. 2. Press the START/STOP button to activate the function, and allow the oven to preheat. 3. In a bowl, mix the butter together with the chopped parsley, chopped chives, chopped thyme, chopped rosemary, and garlic. 4. Place the butter mixture in the center of a piece of plastic wrap and roll it into a log; twist the ends to keep tight, and then refrigerate the mixture for 20 minutes until it hardens. 5. Rub the steak with salt and pepper on both sides to season. 6. Arrange the steak on the roasting pan, and insert the pan inside the oven on position 6 to cook. 7. Flip the steak every 10 minutes to promote even browning until the steak has an internal temperature of 145°F/62°C and the steak is nicely browned. 8. Let the steak cool briefly before serving. 9. Garnish the steak with the butter mixture and enjoy.
Per Serving: Calories 445; Fat 37.32g; Sodium 371mg; Carbs 4.19g; Fiber 0.5g; Sugar 0.07g; Protein 24.87g

Lemony Lamb Chops

Prep Time: 5 minutes | Cook Time: 15 minutes | Serves: 4

8 loin lamb chops	1 teaspoon tarragon
2 tablespoons mustard	1 tablespoon lemon juice
½ teaspoon olive oil	Salt and pepper

1. Select the AIRFRY function, and adjust the temperature at 225°F/105°C and set the time for 15 minutes. 2. Press the START/STOP button to activate the function, and allow the oven to preheat. 3. Mix the olive oil, tarragon, lemon juice, and mustard in a bowl. 4. Rinse and drain the lamb chops, and then pat them dry. 5. Brush the lamb chops with the mustard-herb mixture. 6. Arrange the lamb chops evenly in the air fryer basket. Then insert into the preheated oven on position 3. 7. Cook the meat for 15 minutes for medium-rare, flipping once halfway through cooking. 8. Carefully remove from the oven. 9. Serve and enjoy!
Per Serving: Calories 198; Fat 8.6g; Sodium 174mg; Carbs 1.16g; Fiber 0.5g; Sugar 0.17g; Protein 27.54g

Short Beef Ribs

Prep Time: 10 minutes | Cook Time: 8 hours | Serves: 6

6 pounds of beef short ribs	whole-grain mustard
1 pinch salt	1 tablespoon garlic, chopped
1 teaspoon liquid crab boil	½ cup onions, chopped
14 ounces ketchup	¼ cup firmly packed light brown sugar
12 ounces of light beer	1 dash of hot pepper sauce
1 tablespoon molasses	1 dash Worcestershire sauce
1 pinch freshly ground black pepper	1 pinch of ground cayenne pepper
1 tablespoon Creole or	1 tablespoon fresh ginger, peeled and grated

1. Select the SLOW COOK function, and adjust the temperature at HI and set the time for 8 minutes. 2. Press the START/STOP button to activate the function, and allow the oven to preheat. 3. Rub the ribs with salt and black pepper, and then place in the roasting pan. 4. Process together the ketchup, mustard, beef, onions, garlic, hot pepper sauce, Worcester sauce, ground cayenne pepper, 1 teaspoon black pepper, molasses, 1 teaspoon salt, light beer, ginger, and crab boil in a food processor. Blend them for 15 seconds until smooth. 5. Pour the sauce mixture over the ribs, cover the pan and insert the pan inside the oven on position 8. 6. When the cooking time is up, carefully remove it from the oven. 7. Serve the ribs with sauce. Enjoy!
Per Serving: Calories 926; Fat 44.39g; Sodium 1136mg; Carbs 39.31g; Fiber 0.8g; Sugar 29.69g; Protein 95.61g

Simple Lamb Chops

Prep Time: 15 minutes | Cook Time: 35 minutes | Serves: 4

1-quart buttermilk
¼ cup hot sauce
3 tablespoons garlic, minced
2 teaspoons celery salt
2⅓ teaspoons salt, divided
2⅓ teaspoons black pepper, divided

4 lamb chops,
4 eggs
½ cup milk
4 cup flour

1. Select the AIRFRY function, and adjust the temperature at 400°F/200°C and set the time for 35 minutes. 2. Press the START/STOP button to activate the function, and allow the oven to preheat. 3. In a mixing bowl, add hot sauce, buttermilk, garlic, celery salt, 2 teaspoons of salt, and 1 teaspoon of black pepper, and stir them well. 4. Evenly coat the lamb chops with the buttermilk mixture and then leave the lamb chops in the mixture; cover the bowl and place in the refrigerator to marinate the lamb chops overnight. 5. Remove the marinade and let the lamb chops sit at room temperature for about 1 hour. 6. Stir the eggs with the milk well in a bowl. 7. Combine the flour, ⅓ teaspoon of salt, and 1⅓ teaspoon of black pepper in another bowl. 8. Dip the lamb chops into the flour mixture and shake off any excess, then dip them into the egg mixture and lastly, dip them into the flour mixture again. 9. Grease the air fryer basket with the cooking spray and then place the lamb chops on it. 10. Insert the basket inside the oven on position 3 and then cook the food for 35 minutes. 11. When done, the lamp chops should have an internal temperature of 160°F/70°C. 12. Serve warm.
Per Serving: Calories 776; Fat 17.05g; Sodium 2355mg; Carbs 113.08g; Fiber 4g; Sugar 14.54g; Protein 40.01g

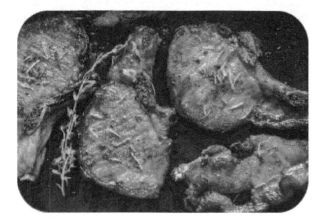

Fried Pork Chops

Prep Time: 5 minutes | Cook Time: 25 minutes | Serves: 4

2 tablespoons honey
4 cloves garlic, minced
2 tablespoons low sodium
soy sauce
1 tablespoon no-salt
ketchup
½ tablespoon sweet chili

sauce
½ teaspoon dried oregano
4 (4 ounces each) bone-in pork chops,
fat trimmed
2 tablespoons olive oil
1 tablespoon butter
Fresh parsley, chopped, for garnish

1. Select the AIRFRY function, and adjust the temperature at 400°F/200°C and set the time for 18 minutes. 2. Press the START/STOP button to activate the function, and allow the oven to preheat. 3. Combine the garlic, honey, soy sauce, chili sauce, ketchup, and oregano in a small mixing bowl. 4. In a large bowl, add the pork chops and the sauce mixture. Mix well. 5. In an oven-safe 12-inch skillet, add olive oil and heat over medium-high heat. 6. Then add the pork and sauce to the heated skillet and sear for about 4 minutes or more, until both sides are just browned. 7. Turn off the heat. 8. Add butter and the pork chops to the roasting pan and insert the pan inside the oven on position 3. 9. Cook them in the oven until thoroughly cooked. The internal meat thermometer should read 160°F/70°C. 10. Carefully remove from the oven. 11. Add fresh parsley for garnishment. 12. Serve and enjoy!
Per Serving: Calories 458; Fat 27.05g; Sodium 394mg; Carbs 10.65g; Fiber 0.4g; Sugar 8.94g; Protein 41.19g

Blueberry Pie

Prep Time: 15 minutes | Cook Time: 45 minutes | Serves: 6

5 cups blueberries	2½ tablespoons cornstarch
1-¼ cups granulated sugar	3 tablespoons water
½ teaspoon lemon zest	¾ teaspoon vanilla extract
1 pinch mace	2 sheets of store-bought pie dough

1. Select the BAKE function, and adjust the temperature at 310°F/155°C and set the time for 45 minutes. 2. Press the START/STOP button to activate the function, and allow the oven to preheat. 3. Whisk the cornstarch and water in a bowl. 4. In the small saucepan over medium heat, add the blueberries, sugar, lemon zest, and mace, and stir them constantly for 5 minutes or until the sugar has dissolved and the mixture begins to look soupy. 5. Pour in the cornstarch mixture and stir until the mixture begins to thicken. 6. Remove the saucepan from the heat and set aside to let the mixture cool. 7. Lightly flour the work surface, and roll out the dough sheets. 8. Place a pie pan on one of the dough sheets. Cut ¾-inch larger around the pan. 9. Press the dough into the pan, trim any excess dough from around the sides, and then add the filling. 10. To make the lattice top, cut the second sheet of dough into eight 1-inch pieces and weave the dough to form the lattice. 11. Transfer the lattice to the top of the pie. 12. Place the pan in the wire rack and insert the rack inside the oven on position 6 to cook.13. Let the pie rest for about 2 hours before serving.
Per Serving: Calories 461; Fat 19.44g; Sodium 314mg; Carbs 70.25g; Fiber 4g; Sugar 22.63g; Protein 3.19g

Typical Churros

Prep Time: 10 minutes | Cook Time: 10 minutes | Serves: 4

4 tablespoons butter	2 teaspoons ground
¼ teaspoon salt	cinnamon
½ cup water	¼ cup granulated white
½ cup all-purpose flour	sugar
2 large eggs	Cooking spray

1. Select the AIRFRY function, and adjust the temperature at 375°F/190°C and set the time for 10 minutes. 2. Press the START/STOP button to activate the function, and allow the oven to preheat. 3. In the saucepan over high heat, add the butter, salt, and water, and bring them to a boil until the butter is melted. Keep stirring. 4. Lower the heat to medium and fold in the flour to form dough. 5. Keep cooking and stirring until the dough is dried out; coat the pan with a crust. 6. Turn off the heat, transfer the dough to a large bowl, and let the dough cool for about 15 minutes.7. Crack the eggs into the dough and mix them with a hand mixer until the dough is sanity and firm enough to shape. 8. Scoop up one tablespoon of the dough and roll it into a ½-inch-diameter and 2-inch long cylinder. Do the same with the remaining dough to make 12 cylinders in total. 9. In a large bowl, mix up the cinnamon and sugar and dip the cylinders into the cinnamon mix to coat. 10. Arrange the cylinders on a plate and refrigerate for 20 minutes. 11. Grease the air fryer basket with cooking spray and place the cylinders in the basket, and spritz with cooking spray. 12. Insert the basket inside the oven on position 3 and cook them. 13. Flip the churros halfway through the cooking time. 14. When cooked, the churros should be golden brown and fluffy. 15. Serve immediately.
Per Serving: Calories 217; Fat 16.36g; Sodium 2436mg; Carbs 14.86g; Fiber 1.4g; Sugar 1.37g; Protein 3.5g

Vanilla Chocolate Cakes

Prep Time: 5 minutes | Cook Time: 20 minutes | Serves: 6

¼ cup heavy cream
8 ounces semi-sweet chocolate, chopped, divided
5 tablespoons unsalted butter, divided

5 tablespoons sugar, divided
2 large eggs, separated, divided
½ teaspoon vanilla extract
1 pinch salt
3 tablespoons all-purpose flour

To make the ganache:
1. In the saucepan over low heat, bring the cream to simmer. 2. In a bowl, add 2 ounces of the chocolate and then pour the cream over the chocolate; stir them for 2 to 3 minutes to combine. 3. Chill the mixture until firm. 4. Form the mixture into six 1-inch balls. Store the ganache in the refrigerator.

To make the cakes:
1. Select the BAKE function, and adjust the temperature at 325°F/165°C and set the time for 15 minutes. 2. Press the START/STOP button to activate the function, and allow the oven to preheat. 3. Grease six 6-ounce ramekins with one teaspoon of butter in each ramekin; pour one teaspoon of sugar into each ramekin, turn to coat, and tap out any excess sugar. 4. Melt the remaining chocolate and add it to a bowl with four tablespoons of butter. Set the bowl over simmering water and stir to combine. 5. Allow the chocolate to cool slightly, and then stir in the egg yolks, vanilla, and flour. 6. Whip the egg whites in the electric mixer until thickened and foamy. 7. Gradually beat in 3 tablespoons of sugar and continue beating until stiff peaks form. 8. Fold the egg whites into the chocolate mixture and combine them well. 9. Evenly divide the batter between the prepared ramekins. Press a ganache ball into each ramekin and cover with the batter. 10. Place the ramekins in the roasting pan, and insert the pan inside the oven on position 6 to cook. 11. Let the cakes cool for 3 minutes before serving.
Per Serving: Calories 326; Fat 22.75g; Sodium 41mg; Carbs 32.85g; Fiber 2.2g; Sugar 26.21g; Protein 3.26g

Cinnamon Strawberry Crumble

Prep Time: 15 minutes | Cook Time: 35 minutes | Serves: 6

6 cups strawberries
1 tablespoon fresh lemon juice
2 tablespoons all-purpose flour
3 tablespoons light brown sugar, divided
⅓ cup almond flour
⅓ cup rolled oats

½ teaspoon baking powder
½ teaspoon cinnamon
⅛ teaspoon salt
3 tablespoon cold unsalted butter, cut into pieces

1. Select the BAKE function, and adjust the temperature at 375°F/190°C and set the time for 35 minutes. 2. Press the START/STOP button to activate the function, and allow the oven to preheat. 3. Lightly grease the roasting pan with cooking spray. 4. Layer the strawberries on the bottom of the pan and toss them with lemon juice. 5. In a small mixing bowl, combine the flour and one tablespoon of light brown sugar; mix until incorporated. 6. Add the brown sugar mixture to the strawberries and mix to combine. Set aside. 7. Mix up the almond flour, oats, baking powder, cinnamon, salt, and the remaining brown sugar in the mixing bowl. 8. Rub in the butter until the mixture is crumbly. 9. Press the mixture between your fingers into small lumps and sprinkle over the strawberries. 10. Bake the food for 30 to 35 minutes on position 6 until the top is golden brown and the fruit is bubbling. 11. Remove the food from the oven and let stand for a few minutes.
Per Serving: Calories 111; Fat 4.72g; Sodium 57mg; Carbs 18.5g; Fiber 3.9g; Sugar 8.65g; Protein 2.39g

Caramelized Peaches

Prep Time: 10 minutes | Cook Time: 15 minutes | Serves: 4

2 tablespoons sugar
¼ teaspoon ground cinnamon

4 peaches, each cut in half
Cooking spray

1. Select the AIRFRY function, and adjust the temperature at 350°F/175°C and set the time for 10 minutes. 2. Press the START/STOP button to activate the function, and allow the oven to preheat. 3. Evenly coat the peaches with sugar and cinnamon. 4. Lightly spray the roasting pan with cooking spray. 5. Place the peaches in the pan in a single layer and lightly mist the peaches with cooking spray. 6. Cook the peaches on position 3. 7. Flip the peaches halfway through the cooking time. 8. Let the peaches cool before serving.

Per Serving: Calories 89; Fat 0.1g; Sodium 6mg; Carbs 23.67g; Fiber 1.4g; Sugar 22.18g; Protein 0.45g

Walnut Pie

Prep Time: 5 minutes | Cook Time: 35 minutes | Serves: 6

All-purpose flour for dusting
1 store-bought or homemade prepared pie dough, room temperature
1½ cups walnuts, chopped

4 large eggs
1⅓ cups light corn syrup
⅔ cup light brown sugar
2 tablespoons unsalted butter, melted
1¼ teaspoons vanilla extract
½ teaspoon salt

1. Select the BAKE function, and adjust the temperature at 300°F/150°C and set the time for 35 minutes. 2. Press the START/STOP button to activate the function, and allow the oven to preheat. 3. Lightly dust a work surface with the flour and roll out the pie dough. 4. Fold the edges of the dough under itself so that the folded edges sit above the rim of your pie pan. Curl the edges of the pie dough to form a decorative edge. 5. Place the walnuts in the pie shell. 6. In a mixing bowl, mix up the eggs, corn syrup, brown sugar, melted butter, vanilla, and salt until smooth. 7. Pour the mixture over the nuts in the pie shell. 8. Place the pan in the wire rack and insert the rack inside the oven on position 6 to cook. 9. When done, the crust should be golden brown, and the pie should be just set. 10. Let the pie cool for at least 50 minutes before serving.

Per Serving: Calories 587; Fat 28.81g; Sodium 411mg; Carbs 82.24g; Fiber 1.8g; Sugar 59.21g; Protein 6.43g

Raisin Apple Dumplings

Prep Time: 10 minutes | Cook Time: 25 minutes | Serves: 4

2 tablespoons melted coconut oil
2 puff pastry sheets, cut into the size desired

1 tablespoon brown sugar
2 tablespoons raisins
2 small apples

1. Select the BAKE function, and adjust the temperature at 355°F/180°C and set the time for 25 minutes. 2. Press the START/STOP button to activate the function, and allow the oven to preheat. 3. Core and peel apples and mix with raisins and sugar. 4. Place a bit of apple mixture on the middle of puff pastry sheets and brush the sides with melted coconut oil to knead the pastry. 5. Arrange the apple dumplings in the roasting pan and insert the pan inside the oven on position 6. 6. Cook the food for 25 minutes, turning halfway through. 7. The food will be golden when done.

Per Serving: Calories 235; Fat 15.88g; Sodium 59mg; Carbs 23.08g; Fiber 2.1g; Sugar 10.02g; Protein 1.92g

Cinnamon-Raisin Bread Pudding

Prep Time: 5 minutes | Cook Time: 20 minutes | Serves: 2

1 cup cubed cinnamon-raisin bread
1 large egg
⅔ cup 2% milk
3 tablespoons brown sugar
1 tablespoon melted butter

½ teaspoon ground cinnamon
¼ teaspoon ground nutmeg
Dash salt
⅓ cup raisins

1. Select the BAKE function, and adjust the temperature at 350°F/175°C and set the time for 15 minutes. 2. Press the START/STOP button to activate the function, and allow the oven to preheat. 3. Grease the muffin cups and apportion the bread cubes between them. 4. Mix up the brown sugar, milk, butter, egg, salt, nutmeg, and cinnamon in a bowl; stir in the raisins, and then pour the mixture over the bread cubes. 5. Let the food stand for 15 minutes before baking. 6. Transfer the food to the roasting pan and insert the pan inside the oven on position 6 to cook. 7. When done, transfer the food to the serving plate.
Per Serving: Calories 222; Fat 11.51g; Sodium 218mg; Carbs 25.31g; Fiber 1.1g; Sugar 16.91g; Protein 5.29g

Apricot-Blueberry Crumble

Prep Time: 10 minutes | Cook Time: 20 minutes | Serves: 4

½ cup fresh apricots, de-stoned and cubed
1 cup fresh blueberries
½ cup sugar

1 tablespoon lemon juice
1 cup flour
Salt, to taste
1 tablespoon butter

1. Select the BAKE function, and adjust the temperature at 390°F/200°C and set the time for 20 minutes. 2. Press the START/STOP button to activate the function, and allow the oven to preheat. 3. Mix the apricot with the lemon juice, blueberries, and two tablespoons of sugar in a bowl. 4. Evenly spread the apricot mixture on the greased Baking Pan. 5. In another bowl, mix up the flour, the remaining sugar, one tablespoon of cold water, and the butter until the mixture is crumbly. 6. Top the apricot mixture with the flour mixture. 7. Place the food in the roasting pan and insert the pan inside the oven on position 6 to cook. 8. When done, serve and enjoy.
Per Serving: Calories 284; Fat 3.49g; Sodium 66mg; Carbs 60.88g; Fiber 3.1g; Sugar 34.19g; Protein 4.24g

Easy-to-Make Smores

Prep Time: 5 minutes | Cook Time: 10 minutes | Serves: 4

4 graham crackers
4 large marshmallows

1 milk chocolate bar

1. Select the AIRFRY function, and adjust the temperature at 375°F/190°C and set the time for 10 minutes. 2. Press the START/STOP button to activate the function, and allow the oven to preheat. 3. Place the four graham halves in the roasting pan. 4. Cut a small slice of the marshmallows and stick it to the graham crackers. 5. Cook them in the oven on position 3. 6. After 8 minutes of cooking, evenly apportion the chocolate bar between the marshmallows and top them with another graham cracker halves. 7. Resume baking them for 2 minutes. 8. Serve warm.
Per Serving: Calories 95; Fat 2.99g; Sodium 52mg; Carbs 16.97g; Fiber 0.3g; Sugar 10.94g; Protein 0.96g

Apple Fritters

Prep Time: 5 minutes | Cook Time: 10 minutes | Serves: 4

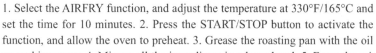

½ cup self-rising flour
½ cup coconut flour
1 cup sour cream
½ cup granulated sugar
1 teaspoon ground cinnamon

½ teaspoon ground cardamom
1 large apple, peeled, cored, and grated

1. Select the AIRFRY function, and adjust the temperature at 330°F/165°C and set the time for 10 minutes. 2. Press the START/STOP button to activate the function, and allow the oven to preheat. 3. Grease the roasting pan with the oil or cooking spray. 4. Mix up all the ingredients in a large bowl. 5. Form the mixture into equal-sized fritters and place them on the pan. 6. Insert the pan inside the oven on position 3 to cook. 7. Turn the fritters halfway through. 8. When the time is up, serve and enjoy.
Per Serving: Calories 219; Fat 6.43g; Sodium 267mg; Carbs 31.66g; Fiber 2.5g; Sugar 18.98g; Protein 3.97g

Pumpkin Muffins

Prep Time: 10 minutes | Cook Time: 20 minutes | Serves: 6

2 eggs
1 tablespoon pumpkin spice
1 teaspoon baking powder
3 tablespoons Swerve

1 tablespoon coconut flour
1½ cups almond flour
¼ teaspoon liquid stevia
8 tablespoons butter, melted

1. Select the BAKE function, and adjust the temperature at 300°F/150°C and set the time for 20 minutes. 2. Press the START/STOP button to activate the function, and allow the oven to preheat. 3. Line the roasting pan with cupcake liners. 4. Mix the eggs, sweetener, and butter in a bowl until well combined, then add the remaining ingredients and mix them well. 5. Pour the mixture into the prepared cupcake liners and insert the pan inside the oven on position 6. 6. Bake the muffins for 15 to 20 minutes. 7. Serve directly after cooking.
Per Serving: Calories 186; Fat 18.9g; Sodium 160mg; Carbs 1.56g; Fiber 0.2g; Sugar 0.39g; Protein 3.29g

Cinnamon Pears

Prep Time: 10 minutes | Cook Time: 25 minutes | Serves: 4

4 pears, cut in half and cored
1 teaspoon vanilla

¼ teaspoon cinnamon
½ cup maple syrup

1. Select the BAKE function, and adjust the temperature at 375°F/190°C and set the time for 25 minutes. 2. Press the START/STOP button to activate the function, and allow the oven to preheat. 3. Mix up the maple syrup and vanilla in the bowl. 4. Arrange the pear halves in the roasting pan, sprinkle them with the cinnamon and drizzle the vanilla mixture over them. 5. Insert the pan inside the oven on position 6. 6. Bake the pears for 25 minutes. 7. When done, transfer the pears to the serving plate.
Per Serving: Calories 157; Fat 0.31g; Sodium 5mg; Carbs 39.66g; Fiber 4.5g; Sugar 32.54g; Protein 0.63g

Cinnamon Apricot Crisp

Prep Time: 10 minutes | Cook Time: 30 minutes | Serves: 6

For the filling:
6 cups apricots, pitted and sliced
½ teaspoon ground ginger
1 tablespoon cornstarch
½ cup maple syrup
½ teaspoon cinnamon
½ teaspoon lemon zest

For the topping:
¾ cup all-purpose flour
1 cup old-fashioned oats
3 tablespoons brown sugar
6 tablespoons butter, cubed
1 teaspoon cinnamon
¼ teaspoon salt

1. Select the BAKE function, and adjust the temperature at 350°F/175°C and set the time for 30 minutes. 2. Press the START/STOP button to activate the function, and allow the oven to preheat. 3. Grease the roasting pan with the cooking spray. 4. Add all the filling ingredients to the bowl and mix them well. 5. Mix up all the topping ingredients and then sprinkle them over the filling mixture. 6. Transfer the mixture to the pan and insert the pan inside the oven on position 6. 7. Bake the food for 30 minutes. 8. Serve and enjoy.
Per Serving: Calories 602; Fat 13.47g; Sodium 206mg; Carbs 127.21g; Fiber 12.7g; Sugar 89.56g; Protein 8.91g

Pecan Brownies

Prep Time: 10 minutes | Cook Time: 35 minutes | Serves: 12

2 eggs, lightly beaten
1 cup all-purpose flour
2 cups brown sugar
½ cup butter softened
¾ cup pecan pieces
1 teaspoon vanilla
1 teaspoon baking powder

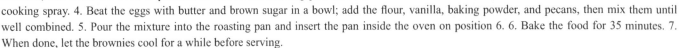

1. Select the BAKE function, and adjust the temperature at 350°F/175°C and set the time for 35 minutes. 2. Press the START/STOP button to activate the function, and allow the oven to preheat. 3. Grease the roasting pan with the cooking spray. 4. Beat the eggs with butter and brown sugar in a bowl; add the flour, vanilla, baking powder, and pecans, then mix them until well combined. 5. Pour the mixture into the roasting pan and insert the pan inside the oven on position 6. 6. Bake the food for 35 minutes. 7. When done, let the brownies cool for a while before serving.
Per Serving: Calories 234; Fat 13.62g; Sodium 114mg; Carbs 25.97g; Fiber 0.9g; Sugar 16.88g; Protein 2.98g

Peanut Butter Cookies

Prep Time: 10 minutes | Cook Time: 5 minutes | Serves: 10

1 egg
1 cup peanut butter
1 cup sugar

1. Select the AIRFRY function, and adjust the temperature at 350°F/175°C and set the time for 5 minutes. 2. Press the START/STOP button to activate the function, and allow the oven to preheat. 3. Line the roasting pan with parchment paper. 4. Mix up all the ingredients in the bowl, and then form the mixture into cookies. 5. Place the cookies on the prepared roasting pan and insert the pan inside the oven on position 3. 6. Cook the food for 5 minutes. 7. Serve and enjoy.
Per Serving: Calories 126; Fat 5.58g; Sodium 396mg; Carbs 16.42g; Fiber 0.5g; Sugar 14.76g; Protein 2.71g

Chocolate Donuts

Prep Time: 10 minutes | Cook Time: 10 minutes | Serves: 8

1 cup all-purpose flour	½ cup granulated sugar
1 teaspoon vanilla	½ teaspoon baking soda
2 tablespoons butter, melted	¼ cup unsweetened cocoa
1 egg, lightly beaten	powder
½ cup buttermilk	⅛ teaspoon salt

1. Select the BAKE function, and adjust the temperature at 350°F/175°C and set the time for 10 minutes. 2. Press the START/STOP button to activate the function, and allow the oven to preheat. 3. Spray a donut pan with cooking spray. 4. Combine the flour, baking soda, cocoa powder, and salt in a mixing bowl. 5. Whisk the egg, vanilla, butter, sugar, and buttermilk in another bowl until well combined. 6. Pour the egg mixture into the flour mixture and mix until just combined. 7. Spoon the batter into the prepared donut pan. Place the pan in the wire rack and then insert the rack inside the oven on position 6. 8. Bake the donuts for 8 to 10 minutes. 9. Serve and enjoy.

Per Serving: Calories 135; Fat 4.56g; Sodium 462mg; Carbs 20.75g; Fiber 1.2g; Sugar 7.2g; Protein 3.58g

Hazelnut Brownies

Prep Time: 10 minutes | Cook Time: 20 minutes | Serves: 8

1 egg	chopped
2 ounces flour	1-ounce hazelnuts, chopped
¼ cup butter	1 teaspoon vanilla
2 ounces chocolate,	2½ ounces caster sugar

1. Select the AIRFRY function, and adjust the temperature at 360°F/180°C and set the time for 20 minutes. 2. Press the START/STOP button to activate the function, and allow the oven to preheat. 3. Grease the roasting pan with oil or cooking spray. 4. In the saucepan over low heat, melt the chocolate. 5. Turn off the heat, stir the chocolate well and set it aside to cool. 6. Whisk the egg, vanilla, and sugar in a bowl; when the mixture is creamy, add melted chocolate mixture and flour and mix them until well combined. 7. Pour the mixture into the pan and insert the pan inside the oven on position 3. 8. Cook the food for 18 to 20 minutes. 9. Serve and enjoy.

Per Serving: Calories 171; Fat 9.27g; Sodium 64mg; Carbs 19.65g; Fiber 0.7g; Sugar 12.51g; Protein 2.59g

Fluffy Orange Cake

Prep Time: 10 minutes | Cook Time: 20 minutes | Serves: 6

1 stick of butter, at room temperature	½ teaspoon baking powder
5 tablespoons liquid monk fruit	½ teaspoon ground
2 eggs plus one egg yolk, beaten	cinnamon
⅓ cup hazelnuts, roughly chopped	½ teaspoon ground allspice
3 tablespoons sugar-free orange	½ teaspoon ground anise
marmalade	seed
6 ounces almond flour	Cooking spray
1 teaspoon baking soda	

1. Select the BAKE function, and adjust the temperature at 310°F/155°C and set the time for 20 minutes. 2. Press the START/STOP button to activate the function, and allow the oven to preheat. 3. Lightly spritz the roasting pan with cooking spray. 4. Mix up the butter and liquid monk fruit in a bowl until the mixture is pale and smooth. 5. Mix in the beaten eggs, hazelnuts, and marmalade and whisk again until well incorporated. 6. Add the almond flour, baking soda, baking powder, cinnamon, allspice, and anise seed and mix well. 7. Transfer the batter to the pan and insert the pan inside the oven on position 6 to cook. 8. When done, the top of the cake should spring back when gently pressed with your fingers. 9. Transfer the cake to a wire rack and let the cake cool to room temperature before serving.

Per Serving: Calories 495; Fat 44.66g; Sodium 341mg; Carbs 19.74g; Fiber 6.1g; Sugar 10.57g; Protein 10.55g

Conclusion

In conclusion, it can be said that air fryers have become a necessity in today's modern world if we consider their agility. It is not just a fancy luxury anymore. A single, compact and simple device provides a variety of functions for cooking food at a very reasonable price. If the features are considered and compared with the price, it appears that the air fryers are easily affordable. The Breville Smart Air Fryer Oven is by far one of the most user-friendly, top-notch, efficient, effective, convenient, and affordable options among all the other options available in the market. It has 14 preset cooking functions available in it which are air fry, TOAST, BAGEL, BROIL, BAKE, ROAST, WARM, PIZZA, PROOF, REHEAT, COOKIES, SLOW COOK, DEHYDRATE, and PHASE COOK. The functions are making life easier by making cooking an easy task. This also provides the opportunity to have life-long access to healthy food. People can cook the food in the Breville Smart Air Fryer Oven and can cherish the memories they make with their loved ones while cooking the food.

The Breville Smart Air Fryer Oven is very user-friendly and simple. It has an LCD panel that displays all the required information to get through all the functions of the appliance. The device also has control buttons to adjust the temperatures, convection, time, and other similar functions before or during the cooking cycle. this gives the user complete control of the device and the cooking process. The final word is that the Breville Smart Air Fryer Oven is the key to a nutritious, healthy, and happy life.

Appendix 1 Measurement Conversion Chart

VOLUME EQUIVALENTS (LIQUID

US STANDARD	US STANDARD (OUNCES)	METRIC (APPROXIMATE)
2 tablespoons	1 fl.oz	30 mL
¼ cup	2 fl.oz	60 mL
½ cup	4 fl.oz	120 mL
1 cup	8 fl.oz	240 mL
1½ cup	12 fl.oz	355 mL
2 cups or 1 pint	16 fl.oz	475 mL
4 cups or 1 quart	32 fl.oz	1 L
1 gallon	128 fl.oz	4 L

VOLUME EQUIVALENTS (DRY)

US STANDARD	METRIC (APPROXIMATE)
⅛ teaspoon	0.5 mL
¼ teaspoon	1 mL
½ teaspoon	2 mL
¾ teaspoon	4 mL
1 teaspoon	5 mL
1 tablespoon	15 mL
¼ cup	59 mL
½ cup	118 mL
¾ cup	177 mL
1 cup	235 mL
2 cups	475 mL
3 cups	700 mL
4 cups	1 L

TEMPERATURES EQUIVALENTS

FAHRENHEIT (F)	CELSIUS (C) (APPROXIMATE)
225 ℉	107 ℃
250 ℉	120 ℃
275 ℉	135 ℃
300 ℉	150 ℃
325 ℉	160 ℃
350 ℉	180 ℃
375 ℉	190 ℃
400 ℉	205 ℃
425 ℉	220 ℃
450 ℉	235 ℃
475 ℉	245 ℃
500 ℉	260 ℃

WEIGHT EQUIVALENTS

US STANDARD	METRIC (APPROXINATE)
1 ounce	28 g
2 ounces	57 g
5 ounces	142 g
10 ounces	284 g
15 ounces	425g
16 ounces (1 pound)	455 g
1.5pounds	680 g
2pounds	907g

A

Acorn Squash Slices 26
Air Fried Potato Pieces 21
Apple Fritters 65
Apricot-Blueberry Crumble 64

B

Baby Spinach Frittata 12
Bacon Wrapped Avocado 22
Baked Crackers 22
Baked Potatoes & Bell Peppers 11
Baked Pumpkin Seeds 19
Baked Rolls 13
Banana Bread Pudding 15
Beef Kebabs 58
Blueberry Pie 61
Breadcrumb-Crusted Flounder Fillets 41
Breaded Avocado Fries 23
Breaded Cauliflower Fritters 32
Breaded Cod Fillets 35
Breaded Fish Fingers 39
Breaded Flounder Fillets 38
Breaded Zucchini Sticks 23
Broccoli Gratin 32
Broiled Corn 9
Broiled Lobster Tail 40
Brussels Sprouts 26
Buttermilk Biscuits 14

C

Cajun Salmon Fillet 35
Caramelized Peaches 63
Carrots & Turnips 25
Chapter 4 Fish and Seafood Recipes
Chapter 6 Beef, Pork, and Lamb Recipes
Cheese Balls 32
Cheese Broccoli Casserole 25
Cheese Fillets 37
Cheese Sausage Frittata 12
Cheese Sausage Pizza 11
Cheese Tomato Halves 25
Cheese-Bacon Stuffed Bell Peppers 10
Chicken and Veggies Pot Pie 42
Chicken Breasts 50
Chicken Breasts with Peppers and Onions 47
Chicken Parmigiana 49
Chicken Pot Pie 46
Chicken Tenders 23
Chicken with Pepper Jelly 46
Chili Tilapia 33
Chocolate Donuts 67
Cinnamon Apricot Crisp 66
Cinnamon Pears 65
Cinnamon Strawberry Crumble 62
Cinnamon-Raisin Bread Pudding 64
Cod Fillets 39
Cornmeal Squid 39
Cornmeal-Crusted Catfish Fillets 38
Crab Shrimp Roll 34
Cream Spinach Pie 10
Crispy Chicken Strips 49
Crispy Chickpeas 17
Crispy Spiced Chicken 44
Cubed Steak 57

Delicious Cauliflower in Buffalo Sauce 30
Delicious Fried Chicken Wings 48
Delicious Pork Chops 57
Dijon Tuna Cakes 41
Dijon Turkey Breast 44

D

Easy Plantain Pieces 19
Easy-to-Make Smores 64
Egg Rolls 11
Egg Toast Cups 9
Exotic Chicken Meatballs 24

F

Feta Shakshuka 14
Flavorful Tilapia Fillets 37
Fluffy Orange Cake 67
Fried Chicken with Peanut Butter 50
Fried Crusted Chicken 42
Fried Mackerel Fillets 41
Fried Pork Chops 60
Fried Tofu Bites 29
Fried Tofu Cubes 26

G

Garlic Salmon 40
Glazed Salmon Fillets 33
Golden Crispy Onion Rings 31
Green Beans and Mushrooms 27

H

Ham Omelet 9
Hazelnut Brownies 67
Herb Chicken Thighs 43
Herbed Head Cauliflower 27
Herbed Rib-eye Steak 59
Herbed Turkey Breast 48
Herbed Turkey Breast and Bacon 50
Herbed Turkey Roast 43
Homemade Cheese & Sausage Burritos 16
Homemade Korean Bulgogi 55
Homemade Potato Chips 21

J

Jicama Strips 19
Jumbo Lump Crab Cakes 40
Lamb Curry Puffs 53

L

Lemon Shrimp 38
Lemony Lamb Chops 59

M

Mac & Cheese Balls 24
Mini Beef Burger 56
Mini Sausage Pizzas 17
Mongolian Beef 56

O

Oatmeal Porridge with Strawberries 10
Onion & Sweet Potato Hash 30
Onion Cauliflower Tacos 28

P

Panko-Crusted Shrimp 35

Parmesan Brussels Sprout 31
Parmesan Eggplant 29
Peanut Butter Cookies 66
Pecan Brownies 66
Pineapple Roasted Fish 36
Popcorn Chicken 45
Pork Ribs with BBQ Sauce 57
Pork Tenderloin with Peach Salsa 51
Potato Pancakes 15
Potato Protein Burrito 13
Pumpkin Muffins 65
Pumpkin Pieces 30

R

Raisin Apple Dumplings 63
Ravioli 22
Red Snapper with Lemon Slices 37
Ribeye Steak 52
Roasted Beef and Broccoli 53
Roasted Chicken Thighs 47
Roasted Chickpeas 24
Roasted Leg of Lamb 54
Roasted Round Beef 52
Roasted Skirt Steaks 58
Rosemary Baked Salmon 34

S

Saucy Salmon Fillets 14
Short Beef Ribs 59
Shrimp-Rice Stuffed Peppers 36
Simple Banana Bread 15
Simple French Fries 20
Simple Lamb Chops 60
Simple Lamb Roast 52
Sirloin Steaks 56
Spicy Chicken Wings 45
Spicy Okra Fries 27
Spinach Rolls 18
Steak with Chimichurri Sauce 55
Stuffed Mushrooms 31
Stuffed Red Potatoes 18
Sweet Potato Chips 20

T

Tasty Cauliflower Fritters 20
Tasty Cheese Sticks 21
Tasty Falafels with Tahini Sauce 28
Tasty Spaghetti Squash 51
Teriyaki Chicken Wings 47
Turkey Thighs 49
Typical Churros 61

V

Vanilla Chocolate Cakes 62
Vanilla Cinnamon Granola 12
Vegetable & Bacon Burgers 54
Vegetable Tilapia Tacos 33

W

Walnut Pie 63

Z

Zucchini-Apple Bread 16

Made in the USA
Coppell, TX
18 September 2023

21702970R00044